More than 150 Scientific Prayers
that will work for you!

Your needs Met

The Healing Nature
of Spiritual Mind Treatment

JACK and CORNELIA

ADDINGTON

DeVorss Publications
Camarillo, California

Your Needs Met
Copyright © 1973
by Jack Ensign Addington

Revised Edition
Copyright © 1973
by Jack and Cornelia Addington

ISBN: 978-087516-490-8
Eighteenth Printing, 2009

DeVorss & Company, Publisher
P.O. Box 1389
Camarillo CA 93011-1389
www.devorss.com

Printed in the United States of America

There is no power in conditions;
There is no power in situations;
There is only power in God;
*   Almighty God, within me right now.*
There is no person, place, thing, condition,
*   or circumstance that can interfere*
*   with the perfect right action of*
*   God Almighty within me right now.*
I am pure spirit, living in a spiritual world.
All things are possible to God through me.

INTRODUCTION

"For thou wilt light my candle:
the Lord will enlighten my darkness." Ps. 18:28

Every problem known to man has an answer. Concealed within each problem is an opportunity for spiritual growth resulting in greater understanding. The problem veils some hidden Truth that must eventually be understood. Once this Truth is discovered, it is as if a door is opened from within through which the student steps into a new and larger room.

It has been said, "where we are tightest, there we need stretching." The Law of Life is exacting. It provides, with uncanny precision, just the growth that each one needs. To us is given a choice; we can struggle with the problem, railing at Life for sending it, or we can bless the growth that it contains and set about to find the hidden Truth that will unlock the door to the perfect solution. It is like a jig-saw puzzle; once the missing piece is found, the other pieces will fall into place. The finished picture emerges.

The Truth that has seemed to be hidden is eager and willing to reveal Itself. "Behold, I stand at the door, and knock," says the Spirit of Truth within, "and if any man hear my voice, and open the door, I will come in to him."[1]

[1]Rev. 3:20

This anthology of Spiritual Mind Treatments[1] is designed to provide the Truth that sets men free — specific Truth for specific needs.

Because most people have not yet learned how to meditate, this book has been prepared to point the way to YOUR NEEDS MET. Each treatment has been instrumental in opening a door of healing for someone. You will find your need included. Your answer awaits your acceptance of the perfect Power within you.

Jack and Cornelia Addington

January 1966

[1]Treatments are written in the first person for personal application. All Bible references are to the King James version.

TABLE OF CONTENTS

HOW TO USE THESE TREATMENTS

Treatment is scientific prayer. It is an individual thought process whereby man's thinking is directed away from the need or problem and put in direct alignment with the divine Mind, thereby enabling him to receive his highest good.

"Our life is what our thoughts make it," said Marcus Aurelius. "As a man thinketh in his heart, so is he," is another way of putting it. As long as man's attention is riveted on his problem or difficulty, he is going to reproduce into his experience more of the same. Through Treatment his attention is focused upon the Infinite, and the result is that he then outpictures his new elevated thinking — infinite Intelligence, omnipotent Power and omnipresent Love. Through Treatment, man is given dominion. It is an open door to all that the Father hath. Through Treatment, "all that the Father hath is thine."

"The Father worketh hitherto and I work," said Jesus. The Father's work is done; His creation is perfect. Treatment, scientific prayer, is man's work. Treatment transforms our thoughts into the pattern of our heart's desire. It is "praying aright". It is the prayer that is always answered.

Words, of themselves, are empty, meaningless symbols. Their only value is the understanding that they bring to the reader, the deep feeling that they convey to the heart. Any prayer or meditation repeated over and over without meaning is an empty talisman, as superstitious a pastime as the wearing of a primitive charm.

> "But when ye pray, use not vain repetitions, as the heathen do: for they think that they shall be heard for their much speaking." Matt. 6:7

The mere reading of the words will accomplish nothing. It is suggested that you read these Spiritual Mind Treatments over several times slowly, meditate on them until you can assimilate them, make them your own. In the Silence that follows, the Spirit of Truth will seem to speak to you.

To find the Treatment that you need, turn to the Table of Contents and select the classification that suggests your problem. For instance, if your problem has to do with a financial need, you might look up the Treatments listed under these classifications: Lack, Prosperity, Business, and Supply. Among them you will find one or more that will seem to have been written just for you. Absolute writings, such as these are, are universal and can be related to your individual need.

When you have found the Treatments that seem to apply to you, read them over slowly and thoughtfully. Meditate on them until they seem to speak to you personally. Study them until they sink deep into your subconscious mind. You will find that when the conscious and subconscious mind agree on these spiritual truths there will be a corresponding change in your experience.

Some of the phrases will seem to belong to you more than others; some will seem to stand out as if they were written in red, awakening in you just the unfoldment that you are seeking. Continue meditating on them until they become truly your own. Little by little, your consciousness will change. Your negative attitudes will gradually become more positive. Where you have felt hopeless and discouraged, you will develop an expectation of good. As your consciousness changes, your outer experience will change. It is done unto you as you believe. Change your belief about yourself and you will change your world.

You see, there is something that you can do about it. Your hands are not tied. You are not the victim of fate. It is a known fact that that which you believe in, accept for yourself, and confidently expect, must become your experience. "It is your Father's good pleasure to give you the Kingdom,"[1] means that the infinite Source of all good is ready and willing to give you that inner dominion that makes all things possible. Read, study, meditate, and accept your good. The healing that you seek is seeking you. It is bound to become your experience.

[1]Luke 12:32

ABUNDANCE

THE WILL OF GOD IN ME IS WEALTH

"But thou shalt remember the Lord thy God; for it is He that giveth thee power to get wealth." De. 8:18

True wealth comes from God. It is a degree of spiritual consciousness, an inner security that comes from knowing the Source of all Good. My true wealth reflects my inner awareness of the presence of God and therefore cannot be influenced by outer conditions or man's opinions. God within is my supply, a never failing Source that goes with me wherever I go. Lo, I am with you always even unto the end of the world of false appearances. There is no lack but lack of faith in God. My supply may seem to come through people but it does not depend upon people nor does it depend upon any certain channel for its appearance in my life. The will of God in me is Wealth, not want, but I must not hinder the will of God by belief in lack, or by telling God how my good shall come to me. Father, I accept Thy Wealth of Right Ideas and let them outpicture in my life as all that I need and more. I put no limit upon my supply for I know that it comes from an infinite Source. Thy Wealth is my wealth. Teach me to use it wisely.

And so it is.

ABUNDANCE

ABUNDANCE GROWS AND BEARS FRUIT

Your word for good renders successful everything that
you undertake. Expect success and you will find success. Your feeling of inner wealth will neutralize any
suggestion of lack on the outside. God's abundance is
your abundance. It flows through Mind into manifestation. Know that God gives you the necessary ideas and
clothes them with all that is needed to bring them into
form. Cease struggling with outside conditions and turn
to the Infinite Source within. The floodgates are now
opened and good is poured forth into your experience.
Think Abundance. Speak Abundance. Dare to give
freely and receive freely. You cannot outgive God.
Declare with assurance:

*My every act produces abundance. I dare to give
freely knowing that I cannot outgive God. As I think
abundance, I demonstrate abundance to the glory of
God Who lives and expresses through me. My business
is God's business and God's business is good.*

And so it is.

ABUNDANCE

BLESS YOUR OFFERINGS
AND THEY WILL MULTIPLY

"Lord I do give Thee thanks for the Abundance that is mine."

(Don Blanding)

I give my offering to God, I give it freely to His work. I give it gladly to my Church that I may share in the wonderful work of spreading the Truth that sets men free.

"Divine Love in and through me blesses and multiplies this offering."

"Give, and it shall be given unto you; good measure, pressed down, and shaken together, and running over, shall men give unto your bosom. For with the same measure that ye mete withal it shall be measured to you again." Luke 6:38

ACCIDENTS

THERE ARE NO ACCIDENTS IN GOD

"Now ye are the body of Christ." I Cor. 12:27

There are no broken bones in the body of Christ.
There can be no break in the perfect flow of Spirit. I
am the expression of the rhythm of Life, one with the
Whole of Life, an integrated spiritual being. There can
be no break in the spiritual body; which body we all
share. There are no accidents in God. Every experience
in my life blesses me and brings me closer to the perfect realization of the One Perfect Life — God made
manifest as me and my environment. If there seems to
be a temporary interruption in the harmony of my world,
I will fear no evil for Thou, the Divine Law of Life, art
with me, healing me, protecting me, leading me ever
nearer to my good. The great involuntary Life which
holds the moon and the stars in their places controls
and maintains my body. I am one with the harmony and
balance of the Universe. I am one with the body of
Christ. I am one with the perfect flow of Spirit. I rest
in this knowledge. I am healed.

And so it is.

ACCOMPLISHMENT

FIVE STEPS TO THE MANIFESTATION
OF YOUR HEART'S DESIRE

1. Dramatize yourself in your mind's eye as doing the ideal thing, living the ideal life, and being the ideal person.
    a. Treat it light. Life's a play and you an actor.
2. Do something about it. "Faith without works is dead."
    Make real plans with assurance (Like packing for that trip).
    Move forward toward the realized experience.
3. Alter the details as you go along; but keep the goal in view.
4. Finish the drama mentally — and then complete it in the outer.
5. Keep the mental image to yourself. Don't let the steam off.
    "Do the thing and you will have the power."
    Do not expose the dream to doubters. They will see the results.

"The Lord will perfect that which concerneth me." Ps. 138:8

ADJUSTMENT

GOD HAS A PERFECT PLAN FOR ME

"What is that to thee, follow thou me." Jn. 21:26

The Law of divine Adjustment starts bringing my life into balance the moment I turn to it. I know that God's Law of Adjustment is operating in my life and affairs right now. God has a perfect plan for me. His Love goes before me and prepares the way for each step in its unfoldment.

I do not depend upon man or man's opinion of me. I listen only to the still, small voice within me that tells me moment by moment what I should do. God has a perfect plan for me and it is revealed to me at just the right time. The Spirit within me knows what is truly right for me. As I follow my own inner Guidance I feel relaxed and free.

I know that I am in my right place doing the right thing at the right time. Each situation in my life is an opportunity to gain in spiritual understanding. What was right for me yesterday may not be right for me to-day. My experience of today will undoubtedly become changed and expanded tomorrow. I am completely flex-ible. I rejoice that divine Intelligence within me is able to look ahead and plan for my tomorrows. I trust God's perfect plan for me. Divine Love leads me and cares for me each step of the way.

And so it is.

THERE IS NO AGE

"And this is the record, that God hath given us eternal life." I Jn. 5:11

Eternal means unchanging. The perfect Life of God is unchanging. It can never grow old, become infirm, weak or depleted; It can never be less than perfect.
   "Birthless and deathless and changeless
   Remaineth the Spirit forever."*
I count myself immortal. God lives his glorious Life through me. I am as young as my dreams. Leaving my fears behind, I emerge each day a new creation of Spirit. Each fresh inspiration carries with it the strength and enthusiasm to carry it into manifestation. Today, I am born anew; new talents, new ideas, new abilities are mine. God's wondrous Life flows through me into endless creativity. I am free, fluidic, and flexible. Nothing can limit eternal Life and nothing can limit me. I am young, vital, and expansive. Eternal Life lives through me as one glorious experience after another. God is always young and so am I.

And so it is.

*Song Celestial
   by Sir Edwin Arnold

AGREEMENT

I AM A TRUE DISCIPLE

"Blessed are the meek for they shall inherit the earth."
Matt. 5:5

A true disciple is one who learns from his teacher and puts his instruction into practice.

The Spirit within me teaches me to agree with Life and eliminates all resistance in me. I willingly and lovingly follow this inner instruction.

As my fellow man senses my sincere desire to eliminate all points of contention, I find that he, too, is eager to harmonize with me.

The Spirit within teaches me to say the right thing at the right time. I am still long enough to listen to my inner Guidance. One good constructive idea after another comes to me from within. I am alert to receive these ideas and put them into daily practice.

I let self-indulgent and self-centered habits die for want of attention. I give my entire attention to the Spirit within and I live spontaneously in a new world of interesting, fulfilling experiences. I am a true disciple of the Spirit, forever learning and receiving Truth. As I agree with Truth, I inherit the earth.

And so it is.

ALCOHOLISM

GOD IS THE ONLY POWER IN MY LIFE

"There is no power but of God." Rom. 13:1

God is the only power in my life. Nothing from without can touch the perfect Life of God within. No past experience has power over me. I am a perfect child of God and nothing that anyone has ever done or said can interfere with my divine inheritance. The Power of God is greater than any circumstance in my life. The strength of God is mine to use.

Turning away from all feelings of inadequacy, I discover that all that I need is within me now. As I forgive the past I find that I have nothing to atone for, nothing to run away from. Casting off the old man, I discover my true Self. I take dominion in my life. Old habits have no power over me. Conditions have no power over me. Personalities have no power over me. I take dominion. I am whole — I am free — I am complete NOW AND FOREVER MORE.

And so it is.

Note: If the treatment is for another, the key is this: We are not trying to make another person over. God's man is perfect. There is no weakness in him. He is not in bondage to false appetites. God's man has never sinned, suffered, or been less than perfect. He is not a sinner to be reformed, hated or condemned. See him as a divine, whole, perfect spiritual being and the strength of God within him will lift him up and set him free. The Power of God is within him now.

9

ANSWERS

GOD IS MY ANSWER

"He shall call upon me, and I will answer, I will be with him in trouble; I will deliver him and honour him."
Ps. 91:15

All things are possible with God. Whatever my need, God is my answer.

As I turn trustingly to the Father within, my need is met. If a choice must be made, if Guidance is needed, it comes to me in a burst of divine Intuition. Joyously I await God's answer, knowing my need is met. If there seems to be a lack in my life, a greater awareness of God's love is my answer. My security is of God. His Abundance is never depleted. My need is met. I breathe deeply of the Spirit and let the Wholeness of Life thrill through me. My youth is renewed. My strength is unlimited. The Wholeness of God is my health. Whatever my need, God is the answer.

And so it is.

ANTAGONISM

AS I LOVE, I AM LOVED

"Beloved, let us love one another: for love is of God; and everyone that loveth is born of God, and knoweth God." I Jn. 4:7

I love the Spirit of God within me. I love the Wisdom of God that makes my decisions and motivates my actions. I love the Power of God expressing in and through all of Life. I love every part of Life. I love the little leaf that is green in the spring. I love the brown leaf in the fall. I love the fruit of the trees. I love the food that I take into my body. I love the air that I breathe. I love the sunshine that warms me. I am not separated from any part of Life.

I love my neighbor and every man is my neighbor. I see within my neighbor the essence of God that is within me. No antagonistic thought or action can change this Love. Love, expressing in and through me, dispels all antagonism.

I love the Lord my God at the center of my being. I love Life and Life returns my Love. Love is all there is and I am part of It. In this awareness I am blessed, uplifted and completely at peace.

And so it is.

ANXIETY

I HAVE NO ANXIETY

"Be not therefore anxious for the morrow." Matt. 6:34

Know that right this moment all of the past is released. It has no power over you. Recognize the mistakes of the past for what they were, efforts to do the best you knew at the moment. All of the slights of the past, times when you seemed to have been rejected, are now released and forgiven. If there was anyone else involved, know that they, too, were doing the best that they knew at the moment. The past is released. Tomorrow will have within it all that is necessary for the fullness of that day.

Let us, therefore, have no anxiety for tomorrow. We know that tomorrow will be filled with Love, with Power, with Good, because tomorrow is merely a further projection of this one moment, and in this one moment we know the Truth. As Paul said, "In Spirit we live and move and have our being." In this one moment we have all the Wisdom that we need. We have the Good that stems from the infinite Source to express in our lives.

And so it is.

BALANCE

I AM ALWAYS IN BALANCE

"Therefore if any man be in Christ, he is a new creature: old things are passed away; behold, all things are become new." II Cor. 5:17
(In Christ means in the awareness of being the son of God.)

In Christ, I am free from false ideas, old ideas of limitation and bondage. No longer do I judge the future by the past.

In Christ, I dare to expand my horizon. Nothing is too hard for God working in and through me. "I can do all things through Christ which strengtheneth me."

In Christ, I fear no person or situation. God's child is one with all people in a happy, wholesome way.

In Christ, I expect divine right action in all of my affairs. God's gift to me is flawless, perfect in its entire nature.

In Christ, I am one with the Father. I am never out of balance. My life is in perfect harmonious adjustment.

In Christ, I accept new heavens and a new earth. I rejoice in my new heaven within and accept my new earth (outer experience).

God is my perfect balanced Life. I am always in balance.

And so it is.

BEGINNING AGAIN

A NEW HEAVEN AND A NEW EARTH

"And I saw a new heaven and a new earth: for the first heaven and the first earth were passed away." Rev. 21:1

Today I begin life anew.
Today I am born to a fresh, new, bright, glorious day.
This new day has never been lived before and will never be lived again.
I enter into this new day with enthusiasm, knowing that the Presence of God uplifts and enlightens me.
I bring into this new day only intelligence, wisdom, peace, joy and understanding.
New courage, new strength, new life are mine to share.
I am adding to this new day new ideas, new methods, new thoughts and new attitudes.
Today I am rich in radiant health, infinite Abundance and Love.
The beauty, warmth, color, protection and comfort of His loving presence fills me with a deep sense of peace, joy and security.
I pour into every moment of this new day the wonderful blessings that abound for me.
My cup runneth over.
This is indeed my day of fulfillment.
Today I am living in a new heaven and a new earth.
Thank you Father, for this new day.

And so it is.

BEGINNING AGAIN

NOW IS THE NEW DAY

"Christ in you, the hope of glory." Col. 1:27

God, at the center of my being, expresses Himself in and through me as the Christ. This is the Truth that lifts me up into the Light and Joy of perfect living. As the seed dies to its old self to rise up into the plant and become blossom and then fruit, so do I rise out of the old darkness. I let go of the old life of anxiety and worry that I may gain the life of Truth. I let go of the life of insecurity and fear that I may enter into the life of God's fulfilling love.

Now is the new day, that bright new day when the darkness ceases to be; the gloom is dispelled, the storm is stilled. Christ in me is the hope of glory, a Power so great that nothing is impossible to It. I turn from my old life of inadequacy and defeat and let God express Himself through me as the risen Christ. I am lifted out of the old into the new creative experience. And for this I give thanks.

And so it is.

BEREAVEMENT

I RELEASE THE ONE I LOVE

"For this is life eternal..." Jn. 17:3

Life on earth is continually changing. We cannot stop change any more than we can stop the clock; yet, there is that within us which never changes. It is eternal in the heavens. It knows no beginning, nor end. It is the same within each one of us — yesterday, today and forever.

The one I love can never be destroyed and is never taken from me; yet, must be freed to God's eternal experience. I release the one I love to the life that never dies. I bless him on his onward journey. I know that he is never far from me and that nothing can separate us in the eternal plan.

And so it is.

BITTERNESS

MISTAKES ARE STEPPING-STONES TO GROWTH

"...Yes, I have loved thee with an everlasting love: therefore with loving kindness have I drawn thee."
Jer. 31:3

Pausing for a moment to look back, I give thanks that the past was not in vain. Every single problem, every unhappy moment appears, from my present vantage point, to have been a blessing in disguise.

But for that lesson in human relations, sad though it seemed at the time, I could never have found my oneness with all of Life.

The days that I spent in bed were actually golden days for they gave me time to meditate upon the Truth of my being. I was forced to reach for a higher level of understanding — and when I did, I found God and His perfect creation included me.

It was when I was out of work and despaired that I began to realize that my Supply was within me all of the time. Transcending poverty I found prosperity but this time lasting prosperity based on spiritual Wealth.

Surely God is All, and evil only my false interpretation of Good. The Lord (the Divine Law of Life) has been with me through each step of my growth, drawing me on with "loving kindness" through lessons I could understand that I might grow to the point where I could accept my good. I give thanks for past growth and press on toward my goal. Every problem is a steppingstone to further growth. And for this I give thanks.

And so it is.

BLAMING THE SELF

I HAVE NEVER BEEN REJECTED

"Thou art my son; this day have I begotten thee." Ps. 2:7

I am not alone. I have never been lost, lonely, or rejected. I have a Father who loves me with an everlasting Love. He is with me always and will never, never leave me. Though my sins (mistakes) be as scarlet, He forgives me completely without a moment's hesitation. As I turn to Him, He comes to meet me. All He requires is that I turn in His direction, seeking to lose my little self in a greater awareness of His Presence. Nothing is withheld, nothing is held against me. All that my Father has is mine. I do not have to beg him for His Goodness. His Wealth is mine to use, His Love is mine to share. Before I call, He answers me. He withholds nothing but wants me to have my every desire fulfilled. Though my earthly father and mother forsake me, He will take me up. Though I make my bed in hell, He is with me, a gentle touch upon my shoulder, a warm, loving Presence within me, always ready to help me the moment I let Him.

I am never alone. My Father guides me, guards me, protects me constantly, and when I listen, speaks to me, saying: "You are my beloved Son in whom I am well pleased."

And so it is.

BONDAGE

ERROR HAS NO HOLD ON ME.

"...There is no truth in him. When he speaketh a lie, he speaketh of his own; for he is a liar, and the father of it."   Jn. 8:44

When subtle error thoughts tempt me, I speak to them firmly: "I will not tarry with you. I refuse to give you room in my house. You are lies and I will not fool with you even in jest. I am not subject to sin, disease, death or defeat of any kind. There is no power in germs, epidemics or my own confused thinking. Get ye hence. I now assert myself and claim my good. As a true son of God, I have dominion over the world and its effects. I live by divine decree. I am subject only to God!"

What can man do unto me? I am in bondage to no one. The tempter, no matter what guise it has taken, can no longer defeat me, once I have given my entire allegiance to infinite Good. Christ within casts out the demons in my thinking and I go free. Error can have no hold over me now or ever.

And so it is.

BUILDING A NEW LIFE

CREATE IN ME A CLEAN HEART

"Create in me a clean heart, O God; and renew a right spirit within me."　　　　　　　　　　Ps. 51:10

O Father, creator of all Life, Truth, and Beauty,
To feel separated from you is death, darkness and
　despair.
Create in me a clean heart and renew a right spirit
　within me.
Let Thy Light shine through my darkness.
I am through with selfish seeking for the loaves
　and fishes.
I am through with endless looking over my shoulder
　for signs following.
It is enough to seek Thee only. It is all that is important
　to me.
Thy Light is the answer to all of my problems.
Thy Truth is my healing.
I am opening my heart to receive Thy Love.
Let it cast out: my selfish aspirations for human
　　　　　　　　　　recognition,
　　　　　　　　my own self-manufactured goodness
　　　　　　　　　full of pride,
　　　　　　　　my criticisms, condemnations, and my
　　　　　　　　　judgments,
　　　　　　　　my resistances, resentments and my
　　　　　　　　　minor irritations.
I would be a clear channel for Thy Light, a better
　instrument for Christ.
I ask to live as a son of God and glorify Thee, Father.

　　　　　　　　　　　　　　And so it is.

BURDEN BEARING

I LET GO OF MY BURDEN

"Cast thy burden upon the Lord, and he shall sustain thee."   Ps. 55:22

I let go of the burden that seemed to be mine to carry. Of myself I was helpless to carry it. It was much too heavy, a futile struggle for my limited strength. As I cast it upon the Lord (the Divine Law of my Being) I am immediately sustained for I lay hold of Infinite Strength. The burden not only becomes light, but like the phantom thing it was, fades away altogether. As I recognize that the *Omnipotent* strength of God Almighty is mine to use, the burdens cease to be burdens. Christ centered, I can say with Jesus, "My yoke is easy and my burden is light."

As I turn trustingly to the Father within Who knows all of the answers and is not limited by thoughts of time or space, ways or means, that which seemed impossible takes place easily. I am relieved of that backlog of "unfinished business" and fresh, new creative thoughts lend wings to my endeavor. "Thine, O Lord, is the greatness, and the power, and the glory and the victory!"

And so it is.

BUSINESS

I BLESS MY WORK

"The Lord will perfect that which concerneth me."
Ps. 138:8

Good morning, God!
This business is your business.
Everything You do is done easily, smoothly and happily.
Everyone who needs to know us is being drawn to us
easily so that you may bless them through us.
We give service, God's service, Love expressed
through this office.
Love permeates this office and is felt by everyone who
crosses our doorstep. Love is our theme.
Love blesses us and all who contact us.
Through Love, all those whom we need and those who
need us are drawn to us easily and harmoniously.
The Love we give away returns to us as blessings
unlimited!
Plenty of happy clients, successful transactions
that bless and please everyone.
Good morning, God!
We're ready to let you work through us today!

And so it is.

MY BUSINESS IS GOD'S BUSINESS

"Now unto him that is able to do exceedingly abundantly above all that we ask or think, according to the power that worketh in us."　　　　　　Eph. 3:20

My business is God's business. God's business is always flourishing. Knowing this, I am blessed beyond my fondest dreams. God gives me the ideas. I carry them out. The result is always successful.

"The earth is the Lord's and the fullness thereof. The cattle on a thousand hills are his." He owns it all and pours it forth unstintingly. God's thoughts are always of prosperity, abundance lavishly poured out and freely given. All that He has is mine as I open my mind to receive it. All that I can receive in the realm of Mind is mine to experience. Life Abundant lives through me. In partnership with God, I cannot fail. My security is an inner condition that is not shaken by outer circumstances. Love is ever replenished from an Infinite Source and poured out to me as all that I need. Customers, clients, ideas and riches of every sort are drawn to me from the One Source. The Power within doeth the works and through It I am in control of my business. My business is God's business and God's business is Good.

And so it is.

CALMNESS

IN THE QUIET OF THE MIND

"But thou, when thou prayest, enter into thy closet, and when thou hast shut thy door, pray to thy Father which seeth in secret; and thy Father which seeth in secret shall reward thee openly."   Matt. 6:6

In the quiet of the mind I find the peace that passeth all understanding. The Infinite Presence of God filling every part of Life is centered within me, my Creator, the Divine Power of Life, the Infinite Love of Life. It expresses Itself into every part of my life right this moment. The Infinite Intelligence within me knows what is right for me, makes my decisions and tells me what to say and do moment by moment. In the peace and quiet of my mind I realize that God is my supply. Spiritual Substance within me is right now all that I need. Divine Love in and through me outpictures as friends and companions wherever I go. As I meditate on the Presence of God within me, letting my requests be made known, my life is formed and my needs are met. In the quiet of the mind, at the very center of my being, I find the peace that passeth all understanding.

And so it is.

CAPABILITY

NOTHING IS IMPOSSIBLE TO GOD

"And God is able to make all grace abound toward you; that ye, always having all sufficiency in all things, may abound to every good work." II Cor. 9:8

Christ in you is able. The Christ is God Almighty working in you to will and to do His good pleasure. Had you forgotten? The Christ in you is never daunted, no matter how great the challenge. It does not matter whether it is feeding the five thousand or causing the blind to see. Christ in you performs the miracles, once you realize that the mighty works are done through Grace. The Power of God working in and through you is always able. Nothing is too big for God. Nothing daunts the Christ in you. When the world seems too much with you, when the goal seems far beyond your human ability, keep remembering:

> God is able to make all grace abound through me that I, having always all sufficiency in everything may accomplish every good work. All things are possible to God through me.

And so it is.

CHEERFULNESS

I REJOICE IN THE TRUTH

"Be of good cheer; it is I; be not afraid." Matt. 14:27

The joy of the Lord, the Bible tells us, is our strength. Jesus continually emphasized the value of cheerfulness. He taught his followers to rejoice, to be of good cheer. When we are cheerful, when we are filled with joy, we are filled with God, for God and Joy are synonymous, just as God and Love are synonymous. Joy opens all the flood gates of the heart and lets God in.

The only reason we are not filled with joy at all times is because we are letting our feelings be governed by outer experiences. Experiences have no power to make us feel sad or happy of themselves. It is only our interpretation of them.

Turn to the Christ within and you will find unchanging joy, joy that is not touched by the rise and fall of human emotion. "Be not afraid," said the Christ of Jesus, "it is I". The Christ, the " I am" within you is your health, your wealth, your perfect Life. It is inspiration, imagination, intuition; it is all that you will ever need. Right within you is this glorious Power — "Be of good cheer." Know for the self:

Right within me is the answer to my every need. Right within me is the Power and Presence of God, my own Christ Self. Right within me is Joy unlimited. I am not afraid. I rejoice in the Truth.

And so it is.

CHILDREN

I PLACE MY LOVED ONES IN THE CARE AND KEEPING OF GOD

"God is in the midst of her; she shall not be moved: God shall help her and that right early." Ps. 46:5

I release my children into the care and keeping of God. Of myself, I can do nothing; but, a recognition of the Power of God right where they are is mighty to help them.

I exchange the poison of fear and doubt for the powerful medicine of Truth and they are lifted up. I trust the Power of God within them and they receive immediate help.

I know that the Truth about my children is that right now they are divine, perfect, spiritual beings, one eternally with the perfect Life that is God. Divine Life indwells them, constantly revitalizing them in mind and body. God Intelligence guides them, telling them all that they should know or do. Divine Love protects them keeping them secure forever.

This knowing on my part acts as a healing agent. I release my children into the care and keeping of the loving Father. I know that they will grow and unfold in God's perfect way.

And so it is.

CHOICE

I CHOOSE TO LIVE THE GOOD LIFE

"Choose you this day whom ye will serve; but as for me and my house, we will serve the Lord." Joshua 24:15

I choose to live the good life, inspired by God and carried out by the Law into faultless manifestation.

I choose health for myself and my family. Casting out all fear of sickness and limitation, I let the Wholeness of God shine through as perfect health.

I choose to serve the Lord, the divine Law of Life in everything that I do. I choose thoughts of prosperity instead of lack and through the Law I experience abundance. I choose thoughts of love and harmony with all mankind and everywhere I go I am met with the expression of love and harmony from others. I choose success and turn my back on failure knowing that thoughts of success mirror success in every experience of living.

I choose to live the good life; receiving my inspiration from the Spirit within, I let it be carried out into faultless manifestation by the divine Law of Life. I thank Thee, Father, that it is so.

And so it is.

CIRCULATION

THERE IS NO LIFE APART FROM GOD

"For I am persuaded, that neither death, nor life, nor angels, nor principalities, nor powers, nor things present, nor things to come, nor height, nor depth, nor any other creature, shall be able to separate us from the love of God." Rom 8:38, 39

There is no life apart from God. There is no over-action, restricted action or confused action; there is only perfect right action. Life cannot be constricted, restricted, impoverished or depleted. Life is eternal, free flowing, on going, unlimited and never ending. Life is Omnipresent. There is no life apart from this Perfect Life.

Therefore, I now turn from false beliefs about my body and the body of my affairs and take my stand for Truth. Nothing can separate me from the Love of God which is expressing in and through me as my life right now. The Love of God is my sufficiency in everything; my health, my perfect Life. Love lifts me up and sets me free from past mistakes. Love releases me from all false concepts. I now turn from the confused life of the senses and find my security in the Life of Christ within. All that I need in mind, body, or affairs flows out from the Kingdom within into beautiful manifestation. And I give thanks that it is so.

And so it is.

COMPANIONSHIP

GOD IS MY PERFECT COMPANION

"Yea, I have loved thee with an everlasting love: therefore with lovingkindness have I drawn thee." Jer. 31:3

The love that I seek in the world is the promise of God within me. God desires to pour Himself out to me as love and understanding on every side. It is I who close the door upon this flood of Goodness by my own acceptance of loneliness.

I now resolve to turn my back on feelings of rejection. I am beloved of the Father and nothing can separate me from His Love. As I find this perfect, all-embracing Love within, it becomes manifest in my world.

God is loving me now as my perfect companion. There exists in the One Mind a perfect companion for me. Infinite Intelligence knows how to bring us together in a perfect way. All that I need is contained in All-Love. God is my father, mother, brother, husband (wife) and friend.

I thank Thee, Father, that Thou hast given me Thyself. I trust You to send me the one you have chosen for me. I rest in Thy Love.

And so it is.

CONFIDENCE

SPIRIT KNOWS NO OBSTRUCTION

"If thou canst believe, all things are possible to him that believeth." Mark 9:23

To realize that God is ever-present, ever-available, is to know that all the wisdom, intelligence and power of the universe is right where you are. It is done unto you as you believe. Change your belief and you change your world.

The answers to your problems lie not in God's willingness but in your ability to believe. Certain statements repeated over and over help you to believe. Gradually these statements sink into consciousness, changing your mental reactions from negative to positive. Say to yourself:

The law of good is continuously operative in my life.

I am always equal to any task set before me.

I am confident of my ability to meet every situation.

The spirit of Truth within can solve every problem, overcome every difficulty.

I realize that Spirit knows no obstruction.

I have implicit confidence in the Spirit of Truth and its ability to operate through me always in every situation.

I am perfect now because I am letting the perfection of God live through me.

And so it is.

CONFUSION

I ESTABLISH PEACE IN MY MIND AND EXPERIENCE PEACE IN MY WORLD

"Grace and peace be multiplied unto you through the knowledge of God." II Peter 1:2

I now look quietly to the Spirit of God within me for wisdom. I let the confusion of the world be clarified through the Light of Truth within. I let the Peace that passeth all understanding dissolve conflict and confusion. I let the Love that flows through me from an Infinite Source be the answer to my every need. I let this Love go out into my life and bring joy to the whole world. I let the Kingdom of heavenly order be established within me by knowing that God is centered in me. Infinite Peace is established in me and rules out of me all confusion. I recognize my dominion as a son of God. I enter into a high place in consciousness where I am one with all Good, Infinite Love, and Perfect Peace. All that the Father hath is mine. God has a perfect plan for me and is bringing it into perfect expression that there may be order in my experience. I rest in His loving care and all is well.

And so it is.

CONFUSION

THERE IS ONLY ONE MIND

"Let that mind be in you which was also in Christ Jesus: Who being in the form of God, thought it not robbery to be equal with God. Ph. 2:5, 6.

There is only One Mind, the Mind of God. The Mind of God is Infinite Intelligence. It can never become confused, deranged, or forgetful. The Mind of God is all-knowing, all-wise, and this wisdom is projected through man's awareness in a calm and orderly fashion.

Every time I think I use the One Mind. I am an idea in the Mind of God and there is, throughout eternity, no possibility of my becoming separated from It.

As I call upon the Mind, which was also in Christ Jesus, wonderful thoughts come through me in an orderly fashion. Inspirational ideas well up within me just as I need them. As I turn to the One Mind the answer to every problem comes to me clearly. All that I need to know is already known in the One Mind and I am an outlet to that Mind. My point of awareness in the One Mind is my contact with God. God thinks through me clearly. I will be still and let that Mind be in me which was also in Christ Jesus.

And so it is.

CONSTIPATION

LETTING GO OF THE OLD, I EMBRACE THE NEW

"If any man be in Christ, he is a new creature: old things are passed away, behold, all things are become new." II Cor. 5:17

Nothing can block or impede the progress of Life, It flows and flows and flows. Nothing can interrupt the process of continual renewal.

With the renewal of the mind, old thoughts are passed away. Letting go of past failures, depressions, grudges and unhappy memories I am renewed in spirit, mind, and body.

Just as I let go of the thinking that is no longer useful to me, so does my body let go of waste products. There is no strain or stress as Spirit flows through me into new, vital expression. There is no pattern of sluggishness anywhere in my system. Nothing can block the flow of Life in an through me. God functions every organ of my body in perfect, harmonious action, letting go of the old, accepting the new — a cycle of daily renewal. The former things are passed away and I am made new through continuous God action.

And so it is.

CONDITIONS HAVE NO POWER OVER ME

"For as the Father hath life in himself; so hath he given to the son to have life in himself." Jn. 5:26

The will of God in me is Life, not death. All destructive thoughts, despair, discouragement, lack and limitation, are thoughts of death and I refuse to give them place in my consciousness. I turn my face to the Life-giving Power of God and claim this Life for myself. God is perfect Life and this Life is my Life now. As I let Life live through me unimpeded by human concepts of limitation, I die to the old self and am born into the fullness of Life. Conditions have no power over me.

And so it is.

COURAGE

NOTHING CAN DISTURB ME

"And to know the love of Christ, which passeth knowledge, that ye might be filled with all the fullness of God." Eph. 3:19

The love of Christ is the Love of God made manifest in me. As I drink deep from this fountain of Love within, my soul is restored and my body made whole. I am filled with fullness of God.

Nothing from without can alarm or disturb me. I am filled with the Goodness of God.

All that I feared is powerless before me. I am filled with the Power of God.

The happiness I sought is hidden now within me. I can never be lost or lonely. I forgive myself and those who have hurt me. I have no regret for the past, nor fear of the future. My soul is restored, my body made whole. All that I need evolves from within. I am filled with the fullness of God.

And so it is.

CRITICISM

WONDERFUL ME!

I am a divine, perfect, spiritual being.
My body is the temple of the living God.
My mind is the inlet and the outlet of the Mind
of God.
I live, yet not I, Christ lives through me.

As I contemplate these statements I realize that if I
criticize myself or another I judge the image and likeness of God. Every time I find fault with my body I am
denying the living God whose temple I am. Every time
I claim a poor memory or limit my own thinking I am
not letting Infinite Intelligence express through me. In
Truth, I am whole, I am perfect, I am free. God lives
through me.
Wonderful, wonderful, wonderful me!
I greet today fearlessly. Love has gone before me to
prepare the way. I greet today confidently knowing God
Intelligence is mine to use. I embrace today lovingly.
Only love goes from me and only love returns to me.
God is loving me through everyone I meet. I can afford
to be patient and kind. I face today joyously and thank-
fully. I let love speak through me in everything I do.
I do not judge others and no one judges me. I am one
with all of Life and Life is one with me.

And so it is.

DEATH

THE WILL OF GOD IN ME IS LIFE

"For as the Father hath life in himself; so hath he given to the son to have life in himself." Jn. 5:26

The Will of God in me is Life not death. We are told that Life Eternal is to know the only true God and the Christ who comes that we may have life and have it more abundantly. All destructive thoughts, despair, discouragement, belief in sickness, lack and limitation, are thoughts of death and I refuse to give them place in my consciousness. I turn my face resolutely to the life giving Power of God which is everlasting Life and Claim this Life for myself. Matter has no power of itself to become sick or diseased. "Matter is Spirit in ever-changing form." Spirit uses matter as an instrument of expression, but is not confined or limited by this instrument. God is the One Source of Life, immutable, perfect Life. This Life is my life now. Yes, "in my flesh shall I see God," as I let Life live through me unimpeded by human concepts of human limitation. The Will of God in me is Life and this Life only will I serve.

And so it is.

PERFECTION IS UNCHANGING

"Jesus Christ, the same, yesterday, today, and forever."
Heb. 13:8

Perfection is unchanging. The perfection of God cannot be altered, depleted, or exhausted. Nothing can be taken away from it or added unto it. This perfection is constantly expressing through man, the perfect creation of God.

Christ, God Life, as man, is changeless perfection.

God is Life, a life that is perfect, complete and whole, yesterday, today, and throughout eternity. This Life, in man, is not dependent upon outer conditions or circumstances. Nothing from without can injure or interfere with the perfection of God in and through man. There is no power in conditions. There is only Power in God.

Man is not subject to sickness and death. In truth, he is eternal Life, a divine, perfect, spiritual being; completely uncontaminated by disease or death. This is the Truth. In It we rest, trusting and unafraid.

And so it is.

DEBT

MY DEBTS BECOME MY ASSETS

"Owe no man anything, but to love one another."

Ro. 13:8

I do not blame anyone for my debts. They were contracted by me of my own free will and through my own volition. Neither do I blame myself any more. I now accept these debts as a challenge to use the creative and constructive Power of God to meet seemingly insurmountable obstacles. Nothing is impossible to God and nothing is too hard for God. I deny the power of seeming hindrances; such as age, or lack of opportunity. I now discipline myself in keeping my eye single to accept the creative intelligence, imagination and power of God to bring into my experience the substance necessary with which to discharge my debts. I have no resentment toward my creditors. I now realize that they trusted me and now, through the love of God, I am fulfilling that trust. These debts now become assets, because through them, I am taught the wonder and power of God's creative life. I am patient and I know that everyone whom I owe is patient with me in the payment of these debts. I am not overwhelmed by the seeming time that it may require in which to pay my debts. I walk with assurance one step at a time and in the depth of my Spirit, I know that I am free now.

And so it is.

DECISION

RIGHT DECISION

"And thine ears shall hear a word behind thee, saying, This is the way, walk ye in it, when ye turn to the right hand and when ye turn to the left." Is. 30:21

There is no problem, no seemingly confused situation to which the answer is not already known to the Divine Mind. In Truth, then, *there is no problem.*

God is the Truth in each situation, perfect right action expressing in my life. As I am made aware of the God Power expressing as Rightness in my life and the lives of all whom I desire to help, all seeming confusion clears away. Right answers, heretofore unknown to me, are revealed to me with amazing accuracy. They come from the One Mind through my point of awareness with that Mind.

I find that there is a perfect solution to every difficulty, a solution that blesses everyone. No one can be hurt when God makes the decision. As I listen to the still small voice within me, I am guided in making the right decisions. The Wisdom of God makes them for me and I make no mistakes. As I turn to the All-Knowing Power within me, the burden of responsibility slips from my shoulders and the way appears clear before me.

Today and every day I will let God make right decisions for me in everything that I do.

And so it is.

DECISIVENESS

DECISIVENESS

I am a decisive person. Through the Wisdom within me I am able to make wise choices. The Intelligence within me knows what is right for me and guides me in making these choices. My subconscious mind is one with the Universal Mind and thus I am assured that all of Life is working with me. In the Universal Mind there is a perfect plan for me and it is revealed to me as I open my mind to receive it. I now accept the perfect answer as it comes to me from within. The Wisdom within me makes my decisions. I trust these decisions. I move forward calmly and confidently into paths of right action.

I am now opening my mind to receive choices. I know that I have available to me a vast storehouse of knowledge, an infinite array of creative ideas that have never been tried before. At my point of use of the One Mind I perceive intuitively all that I need to know. I am guided and directed to make wise choices, choices that will result in right activity in my life and affairs. I now still the mind of all fear and anxiety. I trust the infinite Intelligence within me to guide and direct me into channels of creative activity. In quietness and confidence I receive my strength. I am open and receptive to ideas and inspiration that will multiply my good in wondrous ways.

And so it is.

DEPRESSION

I FEEL WONDERFUL!

I feel wonderful!
The Power of God within me is healing me now!
All of the vitality of Life is surging through my body.
The Presence of God goes before me and protects me
    each moment of this day.
The Infinite Wisdom of God expresses in me as
    intuition.
It guides and directs me into paths of right action in
    all of my affairs.
I am unified with the Wholeness of Life.
I am at peace with my thoughts and with all mankind.
I am healed, blessed, protected and cherished
    forevermore.
I feel wonderful!

And so it is.

DIGESTION

I BLESS MY FOOD AND IT BLESSES ME

"Whether ye eat, or drink, or whatsoever ye do, do all to the Glory of God." I Cor. 10:31

I bless my food and it blesses me. I think of each meal as a spiritual act, an opportunity to glorify God.

In the Bible, the verb "to eat" means to "partake of spiritually, to make one's own." As I contemplate the true meaning of eating, each meal becomes an act of Grace. This is my mealtime blessing:

"Father, I thank Thee for this food which is the outer symbol of the spiritual food, the daily bread of life, by which I truly live. I give thanks for the Word of God which is my spiritual food and joyfully receive its outer manifestation, the physical food which now nourishes my body."

My body is the temple of the living God and His Infinite Intelligence planned it and maintains it perfectly. Both body and food are of one Substance, the only Substance there is. Both are controlled and directed by the Spirit within. I agree with my food and it agrees with me. I bless my food and it blesses me. I give thanks for the Bread of Life and gratefully enjoy its manifestation on my table.

And so it is.

DIGESTION

I AGREE WITH MY FOOD AND MY FOOD AGREES WITH ME

God's perfect Life is flowing through me as perfect health. Nothing annoys me. Nothing irritates me. I forgive everyone who has ever hurt or bothered me.

There is no overaction or underaction in the Kingdom of God. There is only the free flowing action of God. Life flows through me into continuous, perfect expression. Divine Intelligence maintains my bodily harmony, digesting my food without my conscious thought. It takes what my body needs and releases easily what it does not need. I take no anxious thought for my body because I know that divine action is taking place.

And so it is.

Note: It is important to watch to see where you can eliminate any mental irritation, no matter how slight. Irritation with one's affairs, even irritation with politics, world affairs, etc., will sometimes appear as bodily irritation of some sort.

Know that your body is sensitive only to God, infinite Good. Bless the food that you eat. Try using a table blessing before each meal if you do not already do so. Nothing is against you. Nothing can by any means hurt you. Trust and know that the food blesses you. Think of it as divine Substance. Remove any feeling about "bad food" and "good food." The subconscious mind is receptive to such thoughts and will go to work on them immediately. I once knew a woman who became deathly ill if she thought that she had eaten garlic. Many times there was no garlic in the food she had eaten but the thought was enough; she became ill anyway. Change your thought about a certain food and you will change the bodily response. Pray for Guidance that you may be led to eat that which your body requires and then trust and know that nothing can hurt you since God is the only Substance.

DOMINION

DOMINION NOW AND FOREVER

"Now unto him that is able to keep you from falling, and to present you faultless before the presence of his Glory with exceeding joy, to the only wise God, our Savior, be glory and majesty, dominion and power both now and ever. Amen." Jude 1:24, 25

There is no place where God has failed. The divine creation is perfect. God has presented us faultless that we may know exceeding joy.

Today I rejoice in the Wisdom that keeps me from falling, keeps me from lack of faith and poverty of soul, that I may experience infinite Good at all times.

I need not feel guilty that I may have fallen short of His glory in the past. Today, in the only moment that I can live, I open my mind and my heart to receive from the Wisdom within. Letting It live through me I experience the majesty, dominion and power of the Infinite.

In the Silence, I hear the healing word that the still small voice is speaking, "The image of God is perfect. It presents me faultless before the presence of His glory—This is my beloved son in whom I am well pleased." It tells me that all others are one with me, whole and perfect, too. To know this is exceeding joy, dominion and power, now and forever.

And so it is.

EMPLOYMENT

SERVICE IS THE KEY

"Trust in the Lord and do good; so shalt thou dwell in the land, and verily thou shalt be fed." Ps. 37:3

God is love and that love expresses through me as service to others. There is perfect employment for me where I can let God's love express through me.

God is abundance and this abundance is my supply. As I serve life, life rewards me generously. I trust God to meet my every need.

Infinite Intelligence expresses through me as guidance. Turning within, I am guided to do the right thing at the right time in the right way.

My perfect employment is seeking me now. My desire to work is my prayer answered. As I take the human footsteps which are presented to me as ideas from within, I become unified with my perfect employment. In the One Mind I am one with my new employer and my perfect position right now.

All anxiety is removed from this situation for I trust God to provide the perfect way to express His perfect life through me. I give thanks for the abundance that is mine.

And so it is.

EMPLOYMENT

MY WORK IS GOD'S WORK

"What doth the Lord, thy God, require of thee, but to walk in all His ways and to love Him, and to serve the Lord thy God with all thy heart and with all thy soul."

De. 10:12

My work is God's work, given to me to perform in His service. My work is important to God. If I "walk in His ways," that is, if my motives are clean and pure, and my heart filled with Love, then I can count on divine Intelligence working in me to carry my endeavors forward successfully.

My work exists as perfect activity in the One Mind. As such, it is guided, directed, and completely maintained. The Infinite, being All, knows no lack and is never at a loss in any situation.

My first work is to "serve the Lord my God with all my heart and with all my soul." As I do this, I see God (Good) in everyone and every situation. I trust God in everyone and every situation. I praise God in everyone and every situation and everything I do is prospered. As I dedicate my work to God, His perfect plan unfolds before me step by step. God works through me "to will and to do His good pleasure." Every challenge becomes an opportunity to glorify God. No assignment is too hard for the Mighty Power working in me. My work is God's work and therefore it is done easily and harmoniously by the Father within.

And so it is.

LOVE FREES ME

"If ye keep my commandments, ye shall abide in my love; even as I have kept my Father's commandments, and abide in his love." Jn. 15:10

I cannot afford to separate myself in thought from another living soul. To do so is to separate myself from God. I forgive and release. I love that I may be like the Father, Love individualized into perfect experience.

If there is a condition of lack or poverty anywhere in my affairs, I know there is a lack of love somewhere in my thinking. Perhaps I have secretly wished ill to someone by having a thought of righteous indignation, judgment, or condemnation. I can no longer afford this indulgence. I bless them all. My brother's success, even he who has seemed to be my enemy, is my own success. The gift of God is free to all.

I love the Lord my God within me. I love my neighbor as myself. I abide in the secret place of the Most High. I pray for my enemy that I may be a child of God. The barriers in my life are melted. Love never faileth.

And so it is.

ENEMIES

I HAVE NO ENEMIES

"What time I am afraid, I will trust in Thee." Ps. 56:3

Trusting in God, there is nothing to fear. The omnipotent Power of God protects me from those who might seem to hurt me. The enemies have all been of my own mental household; but, there I am King, there Love is the answer. Love disarms the enemy thoughts. Nothing can hurt me when I trust in God; nor does anyone desire to hurt me when Love is my protection.

Once I have won the battle within, I find there is now no person, condition, or situation in my outer experience to fear. "In God have I put my trust: I will not be afraid what man can do unto me."* I have no enemies. "The Lord is the strength of my life; of whom shall I be afraid."**

His Presence surrounds me, protects me, and keeps me wherever I am. Love goes before me and prepares the way. There is nothing to fear. Nothing can hurt me. I have no enemies.

And so it is.

*Ps. 56:11
**Ps. 27:1

ENLIGHTENMENT

GOD IS MY LIGHT

"This then is the message which we have heard of him and declare unto you, that God is light, and in him is no darkness at all." I Jn. 1:5

God is Light within me and in Him is no darkness at all.

God is Light within me and in Him is no darkness of loneliness, separation or fear.

God is Light within me and in Him is no conflict, confusion or congestion.

God is Light within me and in Him is no pain, struggle, or resistance.

God is Light within me and in Him is no lack, no hardship, or loss.

God is Light, shining in every corner of my soul, dispelling any sense of darkness, glowing in every atom of my being.

God is Light, the Light of Truth, teaching me all that I need to know, guiding my steps, setting me free from any possibility of mistake.

God is Light everywhere present, the Creator becoming His expression.

God is Light, the very essence of Harmony, and in Him is no darkness at all. How can anything less than all-Good exist in my experience?

And so it is.

ENTHUSIASM

GOD LIVES THROUGH ME WITH ZEST
AND ENTHUSIASM

"Whatsoever ye do, do it heartily, as to the Lord, and not unto men." Col. 3:23

I look away from the false appearances of the moment. There is no lack but a lack of faith in God.

God is Life and that Life expresses through me as radiant health, zest for living and all of the vitality that I need to put my plans into action.

God is Love and that Love expresses through me as service to others. God gives through me to his other children and the giving makes me happy.

God is Abundance, and this Abundance is my supply. As I serve Life, it rewards me generously. I trust God to meet my every need.

God is Infinite Intelligence, and this Intelligence expresses through me as Guidance. As I turn to the Perfect Intelligence within me, I am guided to do the right thing in the right way.

I trust God to provide the perfect way to express His Perfect Life through me. God lives through me with zest and enthusiasm.

And so it is.

ENTHUSIASM

I AM A STRONG, VITAL PERSON

"Whatsoever thy hand findeth to do, do it with thy might." Ec. 9:10

I am God, Life, expressing as _____(Your name here)_____.
I am a strong, vital person and everything I do is important to God.

I look upon each day with enthusiasm, knowing that it contains some wonderful work I can perform for God.

All of the Infinite Intelligence is mine to call upon.

All of the strength of the universe is mine to use.

Divine Love flows through me to everyone I meet.

I am here that I may use this intelligence, strength, and love to help others and glorify God.

Today I will let my light shine that everyone I meet will be blessed and inspired to lead a fuller, richer life.

My life is important and I am important to life.

And for this I give thanks.

And so it is.

ENVY

ENVY HAS NO PLACE IN MY LIFE

"Let us walk honestly, as in the day...not in strife and envying." Ro. 13:13

A little envy seems to be natural and innocent. It is like a wolf in sheep's clothing. The dictionary says that envy is chagrin, mortification, discontent or uneasiness at the sight of another's excellence or good fortune, accompanied with some degree of hatred and a desire to possess equal advantages. When one envies the good that another enjoys, he is overlooking or despising his own good. There can be no love where envy is, therefore envy is destructive.

Now, I am knowing that envy has no place in my life. I rejoice at the good fortune of another. I like to see my fellow man excel at whatever he undertakes. I am now free to devote my time to doing constructive, creative and loving things, using the very Power and Intelligence of God within me, which is within my fellow man. All that I need is given to me, as "It is my Father's good pleasure to give me the Kingdom," and "All that the Father hath is mine." I do not want what another has, but it is my good pleasure to pass along that which I have to others that we may all share in God's infinite Abundance.

And so it is.

EYESIGHT

GOD IS MY PERFECT SIGHT

"Blessed are your eyes, for they see," Matt. 13:16

God is my perfect sight. God sees through me. I bless my eyes for they are God's instruments for seeing. In Spirit, I live and move and have my being. My physical senses are an activity of the One Mind which lives in me. God sees through me that which He wishes to see — the Eternal Good. As I behold the face of God, that which is Good, that which is Truth, that which is of God, my sight is restored. There is now no imperfection in me, for in Truth I am perfect as the Father in heaven is perfect. Keeping the eye single my whole body is full of Light. I let God see through me easily and harmoniously that which is beautiful, enduring and true. God is my perfect sight. God sustains my vision and I am made whole.

And so it is.

EYESIGHT

I ACCEPT PERFECT VISION

"The father that dwelleth in me, he doeth the works."
Jn. 14:10

Of myself I do nothing; the God Power dwelling in me does the seeing. My eyes are God's eyes — perfect instruments for clear seeing. God sees through me as part of the wonderful Involuntary Life within me. I am relaxed in my seeing for I know that no responsibility rests with me. I direct my attention to that which I wish to see and through the action of the wonderful Intelligence within me, a perfect picture is registered on a screen in my mind. I bless my body so wonderfully planned. It is Spirit in form — "the temple of the living God." My eyes are the windows of my soul. The soul is consciousness. My eyes admit perfect pictures to my consciousness. I bless my eyes for the wonderful servants they are. I relax and release them to God and let God see through me the myriad forms of His creation. I thank Thee, Father, for my perfect vision.

And so it is.

THAT I MAY KNOW THE TRUTH

"But the Comforter, whom the Father will send in my name, he shall teach you all things." Jn. 14:26

Jesus had already referred to this Comforter as "The Spirit of Truth" which would guide us into all Truth.

Let us today set aside all pride and humbly ask that the Spirit of Truth teach us all that we need to know.

Father, whatever it is in my thinking that is causing me to feel separated from Good, whatever darkness in my consciousness that is manifesting itself in this seeming illness in my body, I know it is not of Thee. It has no power in my life. I would see my secret sins (mistakes) revealed to me and know the Truth about them that sets me free.

"God is Light and in Him is no darkness at all." I am now ready to let that Light shine in the dark places in my life, illuminating them once and for all, that I may express more Truth in my life. I am willing to see all my little hates and fears, prejudices and irritations, brought into the Light and clarified. I would be guided into all Truth. I would know Thee only. I would be healed first within, that I may express Thee better in my outer life.

And so it is.

FACING LIFE

NOTHING CAN STAND IN THE WAY OF TRUTH

"As I was with Moses, so I will be with thee: I will not
fail thee, nor forsake thee." Joshua 1:5

The "cloud by day" and "pillar of fire by night" may
appear in different forms, but God's Guidance and Protection are with me every moment of the day and of
the night.

There is no power in conditions. There is no power in
personality. Even my own misguided thinking can no
longer hurt me for I know it is false. I turn to infinite
Wisdom within for clarification. Truth is revealed to me
and this Truth is my healing. God speaks to me, in my
own mind, as He did to Moses and the prophets of old.
Sometimes Guidance comes through something I read
or the spoken word of others. I no longer resist criticism. It may be God speaking to me through one of His
other children. Nothing can stand in the way of Truth.
It cuts through my mistaken thinking as a strong light
pierces the darkness. I am willing to have the Truth revealed to me though it shatter my ego. "Thy rod and thy
staff they comfort me." I accept correction. I rejoice
in discipline. I am glad to give up all negative thinking.
God alone has Power over me. This Power is Love. It
will not fail me or forsake me.

And so it is.

FAILURE

THERE IS NO FAILURE

"I am the ressurection, and the life: he that believeth in me, though he were dead, yet shall he live." Jn. 11:25

Today I am willing to die to the old that I may be re-surected into the new. I no longer identify myself with old, morbid appearances. I cease to live in the past or let its memories have power over me. "In Christ I am a new creation." Christ Truth within me sets me free from erroneous thinking and past mistakes. Today is a new day, bright and clean and without blemish. I choose to keep it that way. No ugliness in the past can deface it. I let the Power within me lift me up into a new degree of livingness. I am vital and alive with an infinite Intelligence to draw upon. There is no failure in the Mind of God. I let the Mind of God think through me. The world and its effects are under my feet. I am ressurected into a new life.

And so it is.

FAITH

I DARE TO BELIEVE

"And if ye ask anything in my name, I will do it."
                                          Jn. 14:14

I ask my heart's desire in the name (nature) of the Christ. I ask as Jesus asked, knowing without a single doubt, that "I and the Father are one; but, the Father is greater than I." I know that the Infinite Power of Life pours Itself out through my point of awareness fulfilling the word of Truth that I speak. I know, as Jesus knew, that the loving Intelligence within me "hast heard me" and "hearest me always." Today I will dare to believe, as Jesus did, that I am the beloved son of God, heir to the Kingdom of God. My every need is fulfilled by a loving Father who is my Feeder, Provider and Protector. My Father is always available, ready to provide me with loaves and fishes, if need be, healing for myself and others, through the inspiration of His word which accomplishes all things. "Father, I thank Thee, that no word from Thee is void of power. I thank Thee that Thou dost confirm Thy word with signs following." I thank Thee for the faith of Jesus. I shall never doubt again.

And so it is.

WE ARE UNITED IN LOVE

"Behold, how good and how pleasant it is for brethren to dwell together in unity." Ps. 133:1

Each member of our family is a creative expression of God; each one respects the creative expression of the other. Each member of the family loves the other, each understands the other. Our family is filled with peace. We stand poised in the sight of God.

God expresses Love through this family as understanding.

God expresses Joy through this family as fun and laughter.

God expresses Abundance through this family. God is our supply and our needs are always met. We are prospered in all that we do because we look to God as the Source of our supply.

We share joyfully with each other because we recognize God as the Center and Source of our life. We worship God together with a sense of joy and assurance.

The Love of God in and through our family unites us and brings us peace and an awareness of the fullness of life.

And so it is.

FATIGUE

GOD IS MY HEALTH

"I live, yet not I, but Christ liveth in me..." Gal. 2:20

I, (state name), am a divine, perfect spiritual being. I am pure Spirit stepped down into visible manifestation. My body is the temple of the living God. Every atom of my being is vibrant with God Life. Only my own concept of this Life can become limited for Life Itself is invariable, changeless and eternal. Any physical weakness I may experience is but a reflection of my own false thinking conceived in the erroneous belief that I have become separated from the perfection of God Life.

I now turn from the mistaken thinking of the past and see myself as the expression of God, perfect as the Father is perfect. There is but One Life and this Life cannot decay or disintegrate. Recognizing this Life as my life now, I let It revitalize every atom, every cell, every tissue, every organ in my body. There is no power in matter. All Power belongs to God and this Power is released through my own acceptance of it. I am now letting go and letting God heal me in His perfect way. I give thanks for my healing and it is so.

And so it is.

FEAR

PRINCIPLE TRIUMPHS OVER CIRCUMSTANCES

"Sing ye to the Lord, for He hath triumphed gloriously."
Ex. 15:21

The Christ Principle within me overcomes every unhappy situation in my life. I do not have to manipulate it. I do not have to make it work. Of myself I do nothing, the Principle of Truth within me doeth the works.

I do not have to seek wealth or make wealth come to me. The Principle of Christ within me is my wealth.

I do not have to find health. The Principle of Christ within me is my perfect health.

I do not fear myself. I do not fear others. The Principle of Christ within me unites me with every part of Life. Through Christ I am lifted up until I draw all men unto me.

I do not fear circumstances or conditions. The Principle of Christ within me is the perfect right action of God in which there is no variableness. I have nothing to fear. Principle triumphs over circumstances.

And so it is.

FEAR

WALKING WITH GOD

"Thou wilt keep him in perfect peace, whose mind is stayed on thee: because he trusteth in thee." Isa. 26:3

I'm walking with God and I'm unafraid.
I'm poised in His Presence, each step is secure.
His warm loving Presence surrounds me—how can I fear?
I rest on the everlasting arms in quiet confidence.
I move serenely through life.
At the center of my being, Life is always in balance.
I am drawn forward from this center as if by an invisible thread, therefore I am always in perfect balance.
I step forward in faith, trusting and knowing Divine Love upholds me each step of the way.
I'm walking with God, poised in His Presence, secure and unafraid.

And so it is.

FORGIVING OTHERS

RELEASING OTHERS I AM RELEASED

"And when ye stand praying, forgive, if ye have aught against any; that your Father also which is in heaven may forgive you." Mk. 11:25

Turning from the problems and cares of the day, I now consciously accept the Truth about God and myself. I know that God is the only Power and the only Presence. I know that I am the expression of God and that all the Father hath is mine. I am a divine, perfect, spiritual being, forever one with my Source. Turning from problems, I listen in the Silence for God's perfect answers. Turning from confusion, I accept the Peace that passeth all understanding. I let the perfect Life of God live through me.

I now release all those who have ever hurt or offended me. I forgive them completely. I forgive myself for the mistakes of the past. Releasing others, I am released. Love is the answer to my every need.

All that I need or desire is right within me. In this moment of Silence the work is done. The Spirit within me is the Substance of all my desires, I joyously and thankfully accept the good I desire for myself and the good I desire for others. That which I realize in the invisible becomes manifest in my world. Forgiveness has opened the door to divine right action in my world.

And so it is.

FORGIVING THE SELF

I FORGIVE MYSELF

"Neither do I condemn thee: go and sin no more."

Jn. 8:11

Any sense of separation from God is a sin. I have made many mistakes in the past. I have "sinned" against myself and others. To continue to have remorse and guilt over these mistakes is to continue to separate myself from God. This is the greatest mistake of all.

I now forgive myself for every past mistake. All condemnation is released. I give up every destructive feeling about the past, every feeling of separateness. I let go of all resentment, every hate, and fear. God knows nothing about sin for He did not create it. The Christ within me has never been contaminated. In Truth, I have never been separated from God for a single instant.

Divine Love at the center of my being frees me from any sense of condemnation of myself and others. As I forgive, I am freely forgiven. I am made free through the Christ. "In Christ I am a new creation." I let go of the past. I have no guilt regarding the past and no apprehension for the future. I am free.

And so it is.

FREEDOM

A NEW DIMENSION OF FREEDOM

"Now the Lord is that Spirit: and where the Spirit of the Lord is, there is liberty." II Cor. 3:17

I turn from all the petty struggles in my world and the world around me. As I contemplate the Infinite, I am lifted into a new dimension of freedom. In consciousness, all that God is becomes mine to experience. That which my conscious awareness embodies becomes my experience.

Turning from fear and discouragement, I contemplate God as Love, a Love that will never leave me nor forsake me, a Love that is infinite and everywhere present. Love desires my highest good and perfects all that concerns me. Love comforts me, forgives me, and restores my soul. Love is the answer to my every need. As I contemplate Love, it flows forth to my experience and every moment is blessed.

Turning from any sense of lack or inadequacy, I contemplate God as Life. The earth is the Lord's and the fullness thereof. In the fullness of Life I live and naught is denied me. Nothing can limit Life as It lives through me. Life is never used up. Life never dies. Life is complete and perfect and this Life is my life to live.

Contemplating God, I contemplate my own true self made in the image and likeness of God. I am an expression of the Infinite and as I let it live through me, all problems are dissolved.

And so it is.

FUTILITY

LIFE HAS MEANING AND PURPOSE

"For as the heavens are higher than the earth, so are my ways higher than your ways, and my thoughts than your thoughts." Isa. 55:9

When I stand and look at the changing world in which I live, I often feel inadequate. All seems to be futile. Then, I must realize that I am one with the greater Life, which is God. I stand at the door of my mind and admit only God's thoughts. Every thought which my heavenly Father hath not planted shall be rooted up and in its place a good thought planted. I let God's thoughts, expressing through the doorway of my mind, cast out all negative thinking which has poisoned my mind and affairs.

God's thoughts are of Love. I let them pour in to cleanse me of past resentment and future fears. I have no regrets for the past and no fear for the future.

God's thoughts are of Wholeness and Life more abundant. I let them pour in, casting out weak thoughts of limited vitality or inadequacy. The Almighty Power of God rebuilds my life and I am made whole.

Life's real meaning and purpose is revealed to me as God's Truth pours into my mind and heart.

And so it is.

GETTING ALONG WITH OTHERS

THE CHRIST IN ME IS THE CHRIST IN YOU.

"...I am in my Father and ye in me and I in you."

Jn. 14:20

As I recognize that the Christ within me is the Christ within you, it is as if to say: the Love, Life, Intelligence, Goodness, and Peace of God within me, salutes the Love, Life, Intelligence, Goodness and Peace of God within you. I automatically dissolve in my consciousness and yours any thought of discord, any hint of the less than Good. In Christ we become brothers, branches of the same vine, partaking of the same Substance, one in the Spirit. Because I trust the Christ Self of every man, I trust Life to bring me my highest good. Because I love the Christ in every man, I love all men and that love returns to me enriched a thousandfold. As I unify with the Christ in every man I unify with all of Life and in that sense of Wholeness I find that I am whole and the thoughts with which I once contended have no power to disturb me.

The Christ in me salutes the Christ in you and we are One.

And so it is.

GETTING ALONG WITH OTHERS

THE FATHER AND I ARE ONE

"That they all may be one; as thou, Father, art in me, and I in Thee." Jn. 17:21

Each person in my life is God expressing at his level of awareness. I may not understand them, but this I know: To reject anyone is to reject God. To feel separated from anyone is to feel separated from Life. A sense of separation from Life results in bodily disturbance and all sorts of confusion in my life and affairs which I do not like and cannot afford.

I now consciously unify myself with God and His wonderful creation. "The Father and I are one." I am not separated from any part of Life. I am one with all of Life and Life is one with me. My mind adjusts to new conditions easily and harmoniously, and this adjustment is reflected in my body. My body is the house that my consciousness builds. It is the expression of peaceful, harmonious, loving thoughts. I am at peace with the world. I cannot be upset or distraught. I am one with all of Life in its various forms. I judge no one and no one judges me. The peace of God is my peace for the Father and I are one.

And so it is.

GUIDANCE

THE LIGHT THAT NEVER FAILS

"Thy word is a lamp unto my feet, and a light unto my path." Ps. 119:105

God is the Light that never fails.
His Wisdom guides me each step of the way.
When I feel troubled or uncertain which path I should take, I put my hand in His and await instructions.
His Guidance never fails to come.
As I listen, the Voice within me becomes my unerring Guide.
No matter how confused I have let my life become,
There is a perfect solution in the One Mind to each of my problems.
Paths of peace and right action are revealed to me,
Loving friends come into my life just when I need them.
New Ideas are born as divine Inspiration within me;
With them comes all that I need to bring them to a happy conclusion.
His word is "a lamp unto my feet and a light unto my path."

And so it is.

GUIDANCE

THE SPIRIT OF GOD SPEAKS THROUGH ME

"For it is not ye that speak, but the spirit of your Father that speaketh in you." Matt. 10:20

The Spirit of God, Universal Truth, tells me this day and every day all that I need to know, all that I need to say. The Infinite Intelligence within me places the inspiration in my heart and the words in my mouth. As I turn within for my Guidance, Divine Wisdom speaks through me easily and quietly. The thoughts that come to my mind are loving, harmonious, and creative, according to the nature of God. All stress and strain goes out of my voice for I feel the Wisdom of the Almighty behind me. My every thought is motivated by Love and every word expresses this Love. I trust God to speak through me that which needs to be said and at other times I am content to enjoy the blessed peace of stillness. Before I speak I listen for my Guidance and afterward have no words to retract or regret. The Spirit of God within me speaks through me in a perfect way to bless, to heal, and uplift all those whom I meet today and every day.

And so it is.

GUIDING YOUNG PEOPLE

THE CHRIST IN YOU KNOWS WHAT TO DO!

"There is a spirit in man; and the inspiration of the Almighty giveth them understanding." Job 32:8

How often we are tempted to tell our children what to do. In time, we learn that we cannot put ourselves in another's place. We cannot give them our enthusiasm or our spiritual growth. We cannot always judge the course that they should follow. Their growth must come through them in the perfect way to be received by them.

However, our hands are not tied. We can help in a far better way. Something happens when we know that the Spirit of God in them "giveth them understanding". The Truth that they are seeking becomes acceptable to them when we know for them that the Spirit of Truth within them teaches them all that they need to know. Our spiritual gift to them is of genuine, practical help where they have been confused by our well meant human guidance.

There is a spirit in each one of us, the intelligent Spirit of God, that always knows what is right for us. It gives us understanding from within, the illumination that clarifies our problems. The Spirit individualized in each one of us is the Christ Truth. It is never in doubt for it draws from infinite Wisdom. The Christ in me knows what to do! The Christ in you knows what to do! Divine Intelligence within our young people knows what is right for them to do! This is the Truth that sets them free.

And so it is.

HABITS

HABIT BREAKING

"....thou hast put all things under his feet." Ps. 8:6

Conditions have only the power I give them; there is no power in conditions. God within me knows what is right for me. He leads me in paths of right action.

I know that Principle is not bound by precedence. That which is past has no power over me. I forgive myself for past mistakes.

I now assert my God-given dominion in mind. I establish a new program for myself, knowing it is bound to become my experience.

I am free from all desire for_____
(name bad habit here)

I desire only that which is right for me.

I move serenely through life.

I am not afraid for all is well.

And so it is.

HAPPINESS

MY SPIRITS ARE LIFTED BY PRAISE

"Oh, that men would praise the Lord for his goodness, and for his wonderful works to the children of men." Ps. 107:8

Today, I recognize the Presence of God in everything that I see. Little bird on the window sill, you are God Life as bird; sing your glad song of praise to your Heavenly Father. Little rose bush in my garden, you draw your Life from the same Source as I. I praise you for your ability to give forth God's beauty right where you are. All that my eye beholds is God in form: sky, fields, trees, even the rocks and stones. I am immersed in Spirit as a fish lives in water; and stirring within me, and all of Life, is a Power so great that I cannot even conceive of it.

God speaks to me today through everyone I meet. Everything that I am led to read contains a message of God's Joy for me. I hear only the voice of God. I see only the Presence of God. I feel the Power of God silently working around me.

And so it is.

HARMONY

I AM IN HARMONY WITH TRUTH

"God was in Christ (within) reconciling the world unto himself, not imputing their trespasses unto them; . . . we pray you in Christ's stead, be ye reconciled to God." II Cor. 5:19,20

God is Love, within my heart, reconciling my world unto His own harmonious nature. No matter how many mistakes I have made they are not held against me when I bring myself into harmony with God's true nature which is Love and Truth. God is Love, individualized as the Christ within me, ever drawing me into perfect harmony with His own perfection. The moment I turn to this Perfection, Truth is brought into my life and affairs. There is a clarification in the situation at hand. Immediately, there comes a cleansing within my own thinking, an adjustment in personal relationships and a revitalizing of my physical body. To be reconciled is "to be in harmony with". To be reconciled with God within is the answer to every problem. Once I have put myself in harmony with Peace, there is peace in my world. Having put myself in harmony with Love, the balance of Love is restored in my life. As I put myself in harmony with the Wholeness of God's Life, this Wholeness is made manifest as health of mind and body. I am forever in harmony with the Truth that sets me free.

And so it is.

HEALING INCURABLE DISEASES

THERE ARE NO INCURABLE DISEASES

"Let this mind be in you which was also in Christ Jesus." Phil. 2:5

In the One Mind there are no incurable diseases; there is only the perfection of God. In the One Life there are no dangerous symptoms, difficult conditions, no pain or suffering. The awareness of the Presence of God dissolves these troublesome thoughts and their seeming effects as "a Light shining in a dark place." The Christ Mind is the Mind of God, the consciousness that "all Power is given unto me in heaven (within) and earth (without)" and "I and my Father are one." As I let this mind be in me I am clothed in shining garments (spiritual thoughts) of perfection. I speak the healing word of God with the authority of the Christ. God's perfection is my perfection and shines on all that I behold. "That Light that lighteth every man" illumines my world and the universe. There is only ONE LIFE, the Life of God. That Life has never been sick, never suffered, never been less than Whole. That Life is my life and the life of my loved one. All is well.

And so it is.

HEALTH

I AM WHOLE

"And now, O Father, glorify thou me with thine own self with the glory which I had with thee before the world (of false appearances) was." Jn. 17:5

God, the only Power, is right where I am, and is everywhere present. It is perfect. It is complete. It is Whole. It is Life Itself. I am one with this perfect Life and It is one with each one of us. I abide in It and It abides in me.

I now speak my word for perfect health. It is not necessary to analyze the cause of my condition for I know that the Infinite Power of God is healing it now. The Power flows through me as continuous Life, cleansing, perfecting, restoring the balance of Life according to Its own unchanging perfection. In Truth, I have never been out of balance for I am God's perfect expression right where I am.

Right now I surrender my fears to the Divine Law of Life. I open the flood gates and let the river of Life wash me clean. God's creation is perfect. His Life is my life. I am whole and entire. He "restoreth my soul" and my body is likewise restored. For this I give thanks.

And so it is.

HEALTH

THE WILL OF GOD IN ME IS HEALTH

"The Lord will take away from thee all sickness."
De. 7:15

Yes, the Lord, the Divine Law of Life, will take away all sickness. But, with this promise there is a condition precedent. The Law demands that we do something first—"Love the Lord thy God with all thine heart, and with all thy soul, and with all thy might."

The will of God in me is health, but I must fill my heart with thoughts that produce health. The appearance of sickness is but the effect of sick thoughts. There is no power in symptoms, conditions, or any of the false appearances called dis-ease. As I turn to the Lord, my God, at the very center of my being, loving this Law of Perfect Life, with all my heart, all my soul, and all my might, there is no room in me for thoughts that outpicture as dis-ease. The will of God in me is Health, Wholeness of mind, body and estate and this Wholeness only will I serve until it outpictures in every facet of my life and I am made every whit whole.

And so it is.

HEART CONDITION

MY HEART IS UNTROUBLED

"Let not your heart be troubled, neither let it be afraid." Jn. 14:27

The heart, in metaphysics, is synonymous with our deep, feeling nature. Spiritual consciousness is the awareness of the Presence of God right where we are. My heart is ONE WITH THE HEART OF GOD. Therefore, I know with glad certainty: the Spirit inbreathes me, God beats my heart; in the One Perfect Life there is no over-action, no false action—only perfect Right Action.

Infinite Intelligence within me, having planned my wonderful body, knows how to maintain every organ in perfect harmony. My heart is not troubled, neither is it afraid. My heart is filled with the Goodness of God.

My heart is a joyous heart, a jubilant heart, a thankful heart, a peaceful heart, a loving heart, a heart strong in the knowledge of God. God beats my heart; I am not afraid.

And so it is.

HELPING OTHERS

TODAY I WILL HELP ANOTHER

"Heal the sick, cleanse the lepers, raise the dead, cast out devils: freely ye have received, freely give."

Matt. 10:8

Today I will help another. I freely give of my faith and my understanding in order that the loved one who needs my blessing and all those who share his need may be uplifted, healed, and restored to a life of spiritual wholeness. Turning in thought to the one I desire to help, I speak to him silently:

You are a divine, perfect, spiritual being. You are the Christ, the Son of the Living God. You are the image and likeness of God, perfect as the Father is perfect. In truth, you can never be separated for a single instant from the Father whose life you express. You are the Temple of the Living God and the Spirit of God dwells within you. The Infinite Intelligence of God is in every organ, cell, and atom of your body, operating and sustaining your body in perfect right action. You are God, expressing as your perfect life. You are healed. I now accept this healing for you and give thanks that it is done.

And so it is.

HURT FEELINGS

NOTHING OFFENDS ME

"Great peace have they which love thy law and nothing shall offend them." Ps. 119:165

I know that to be disturbed about one's life and affairs, even for an instant, is not to trust God. I know that God is taking care of me. I trust His loving care in everything that I do. If things seem to go wrong, I am not disturbed. My life and affairs may be seeking a balance but my highest good is sure to come out of the action. I love the Divine Law of Life and trust It in every part of my life.

Nothing can offend me. If someone speaks harshly to me or seeks to take advantage of me, it does not disturb me. My peace is assured, my life is untroubled for I trust in the Law. I dwell in a circle of Love and nothing but love can enter that circle. My awareness of the Presence of God in my life is my sure defense against all seeming evil. In the clear, bright light of Truth there is no darkness or confusion. Nothing troubles me. I do not give or receive offense. Love is the Law of my life. Great peace is mine.

And so it is.

THE ANGEL OF THE PRESENCE

"For he shall give his angels charge over thee, to keep thee in all thy ways." Ps. 91:11

How sweet to think we do have guardian angels, God's messengers of thought ever watching over us. Angels are God's ideas ever being communicated to man. Angels are God's link with man. God's angel thoughts are a very real experience in the mind of man. If you would know more angels intimately, say to the self:

I will let God's angel thoughts speak to me today. I will trust these angel thoughts to keep me in the way that I should go, guarding and protecting me at all times. Yes, "they shall bear me up lest I dash my foot against a stone." They shall protect me in heavy traffic, keep me immune from all dis-ease, free me from all thoughts of lack or fear, confusion or dissension. God's angel thoughts guard and protect me each step of the way. I am never alone. Like Paul, they come to me even in prison. They open my prison of doubt and fear and set me free. They are clothed with shining "garments" (thoughts) of joy and enthusiasm. They bring me Inspiration, Ideas that are straight from the Divine Mind. They are my liberators, my eternal guardians and companions. I invite God's angel thoughts to keep me in all of my ways.

And so it is.

IDEAS

GOD REVEALS RIGHT IDEAS

"Trust in the Lord with all thine heart; and lean not unto thine own understanding. In all thy ways acknowledge him and he shall direct thy paths." Prov. 3:5, 6

Turning to God within for Guidance, I am made aware of the Wisdom of God. This Wisdom is Omnipresent. It is right where I am and I have complete access to It. The Mind of God knows what has not yet been revealed to me. It knows what is right for me and just how to bring me to it. Through It I am irresistibly drawn to just the right people, just the right ideas.

I am led in perfect paths for the unfoldment of my highest good. My good is right where I am and when I become still and cease depending on human ways and means, It is revealed to me. God everpresent is my wealth of Spiritual Ideas which become my supply. Instead of vainly seeking human contacts I will make contact with the One with whom all things are possible. I let my requests be made known to the Father within and wait, in perfect confidence, to be told the ways and means of accomplishment. God is my security, and my success is assured when I trust in Him. I am divinely guided in all that I do.

And so it is.

ILLUMINATION
THAT I MAY KNOW THE TRUTH

"But the Comforter, whom the Father will send in my name, he shall teach you all things." Jn. 14:26

This Comforter Jesus had already referred to as "The Spirit of Truth" who should guide us into all Truth.

Let us today set aside all pride and humbly ask that the Spirit of Truth teach us all that we need to know.

Father, whatever it is in my thinking that is causing me to feel separated from my Good, whatever darkness in my consciousness that is manifesting itself in this seeming illness in my body, I know it is not of Thee. It has no power in my life. I would see my secret sins (mistakes) revealed to me and know the Truth about them that sets me free.

"God is Light and in Him is no darkness at all." I am now ready to let that Light shine in the dark places in my life, illumining them once and for all that I may express more of the Truth in my life. I am willing to see all my little hates and fears, prejudices and irritations, brought into the bright Light of Truth and clarified. I would be guided into all Truth. I would know Thee only. I would be healed first within, that I may express Thee better in my outer life.

And so it is.

INJUSTICE

THE LAW IS ALWAYS FAIR

"Great and marvelous are thy works, Lord God Almighty; just and true are thy ways, thou king of saints."
Rev. 15:3

The Law is always fair, giving to each man the harvest of his planting. As we have believed, it is done unto us. The thought seed that we have planted is sure to reproduce the fruit concealed in its invisible depths. That which we can believe in, accept for the self, and confidently expect is sure to come into our experience. For every cause there is an effect. If we do not like the effects which we are experiencing we have only to change the mental causation which we have established. How better could Life have provided that there be justice for each man?

Turning to the Wisdom within, I accept inner Guidance in planting the seed thoughts that I would like to see reproduced into my experience. Forgetting the loaves and fishes, I turn eagerly to the Abundance within, knowing that my every need is met there. I establish a new awareness of Wealth. As I accept it for myself, It becomes translated into all that I need in the outer expression, and more. "My cup runneth over." Whatever blesses another, blesses me, for whatever is possible for him, through the Law, is possible also for me.

No one can hurt me unless I let him hurt me. Conditions have no power over me. The Kingdom of true dominion is within and there I make my world according to the pattern I select. The Law is fair and just, and for this I am most grateful.

And so it is.

I LIVE JOYOUSLY

"Your joy no man taketh from you." Jn. 16:22

Today I am living enthusiastically, joyously. I am filled with Life. I am flowing with Life. God at the very center of my being is living through me. I greet this day with confidence and a feeling of zest as I let Joy express from within.

All that the Father hath is mine! All of the Intelligence and Wisdom, all of the Abundance of Life is mine to express in my living. This I am doing right now.

Eagerly and confidently I let Life live through me. Thoughts of gloom and despair fade away for they are not of God and have no power over me. Eagerly I step out into this day, knowing that divine Inspiration leads the way and right ideas are mine to use.

God is expressing through me as glorious right action in all of my affairs. There is nothing to fear. Today is mine. I live joyously, enthusiastically, spontaneously. This attitude gives Power to all that I do. I rejoice!

And so it is.

LACK

THERE IS NO POWER IN LACK

"The young lions do lack, and suffer hunger; but they that seek the Lord shall not want any good thing."

Ps. 34:10

It is very evident that lack means the absence of good. Then, how can that which is not, have any power. Lack is the product of an attitude of mind that is not in accord with Truth. In Truth, the only lack there is, is a lack of faith in God. God is everywhere present and is complete, perfect and abundant Life. There is no power in lack; there is only Power in God.

There is manna for today to meet our every need. It makes no difference what that need may be, a need for ideas, for substance, for friends, for wisdom or for any good thing. When we turn to the presence of God and make our need known, that need will be filled. Animals are not capable of knowing and using God's perfect Law of Life, but man is made in the image of God and knows what God knows. He can speak his word and the Law of Life will respond. "What things soever ye desire, when ye pray, believe that ye receive them, and ye shall have them." Mark 11:24.

I do not believe in lack as a power. I have faith in the power of God to provide manna for today. God is Power, all Power and the only Power. I trust in the abundance of God. I live in the Love of God. I seek the Kingdom, then all things are added unto me.

And so it is.

GOD IS MY SUFFICIENCY

"Our sufficiency is of God." II Cor. 3:5

God is my life; sparkling, thrilling, beautiful, wonderful life.

God is Infinite: there is no lack of God.

God is my Supply; my heavenly treasure, my spiritual abundance, made manifest as every good thing. God is infinite; there is no lack of God.

God is Guidance; my everlasting Source of ideas, enthusiasm and inspiration, assurance of perfect right action each moment of my life. God is Infinite; there is no lack of God.

God is my Joy; as I practice the Presence of God in my life, my joy knows no bounds. I rejoice in His Spirit forevermore. God is Infinite; there is no lack of God.

God is my Security; the love of God within my heart feeds me, provides for me and protects me everywhere I go. God is Infinite; there is no lack of God.

God is my sufficiency.

And so it is.

LONELINESS

I HAVE NEVER BEEN REJECTED

"Thou art my son; this day have I begotten thee."

Ps. 2:7

I am not alone. I have never been lost, lonely, or rejected. I have a Father who loves me with an everlasting Love. He is with me always and will never, never leave me. Though my sins (mistakes) be as scarlet, He forgives me completely without a moment's hesitation. As I turn to Him He comes to meet me. All He requires is that I turn in His direction, seeking to lose my little self in a greater awareness of His Presence.

Nothing is withheld, nothing is held against me. All that my Father has is mine. I do not have to beg Him for His Goodness. His Wealth is mine to use, His Love is mine to share. Before I call, He answers me. He withholds nothing but wants me to have my every desire fulfilled.

I am never alone. My Father guides me, guards me, protects me constantly, and when I listen, speaks to me, saying: "You are my beloved Son in whom I am well pleased."

And so it is.

LONELINESS

YOU ARE NOT ALONE

"I will not leave you comfortless: I will come to you."
Jn. 14:18

You are not alone. The Infinite is with you. Divine Love is all around you. Nothing from without can separate you from the Love of God. There is no power in conditions. There is no power in situations. There is no power in personalities. There is Power only in God.

Let us therefore turn away from the mistakes of the past, declaring them powerless to hurt us. Let us turn to the Presence of God that is right where we are, leading us, guiding us, directing us into paths of peace and perfect right action. Let us know together that God is all there is. There is nothing to hurt or harm us, there is nothing to fear. Infinite Intelligence is perfecting that which concerns us. Think to yourself:

I am a divine, perfect, spiritual being, living in a spiritual universe. I am subject only to God. There is only one life, God's life, whole and perfect and complete and that life is my life. In this awareness I am made whole.

And so it is.

LOST ARTICLES

THERE IS NO LOSS

"For God is not the author of confusion." I Cor. 14:33

There is no loss in the One Mind. That which belongs to me is present in my experience. That which the Lord intends for me, nothing can keep from me. Nothing can become separated from me in my experience unless I first become disassociated from it in Mind. Because I know the Truth about myself and my possessions, I am able to release them into the Father's keeping. I am the steward of all that I need; but, "the cattle on a thousand hills are His." I know that it is "the Father's good pleasure to give me the Kingdom." He knows what things I have need of.

I now thank the Father for the article that seems to have been misplaced, knowing that I am one with it in Mind. Divine Intelligence within me knows where it is and is guiding me to it now. Order is the first rule of Heaven. All things are restored to their proper place according to an orderly pattern already in Mind. That which I need is mine in consciousness. As I listen quietly, I am guided and directed in the way that I may claim it. There is no loss in the One Mind; God (Infinite Good), is omnipresent.

And so it is.

LOVE

THE GREATEST OF THESE IS LOVE

"...but the greatest of these is Love." I Cor. 13:13

Of all the attributes of God, Love is the one least understood and most needed to be understood. Love is the answer to every human need. Love transcends all limitation and transforms our problems into victories.

LOVE is the Perfect Power within me and everywhere present in all of Life. Love heals, protects and guides. LOVE makes the plants grow and maintains my body. LOVE keeps the universe in a state of perfect balance. LOVE is the key to happiness, health, and prosperity for LOVE unlocks the Kingdom of Heaven within from which they all proceed.

I draw LOVE from an Infinite Source everytime I consciously give forth LOVE. Every problem in my life is but an opportunity to give forth more LOVE. If people seem to be difficult, I silently bless them until enemies become friends—friends who have caused me to experience more LOVE. If there seems to be lack in my life, I now realize more LOVE, the one true Substance out of which the world and its effects are made. I love and bless that which is mine and silently watch it multiply. There is no problem which LOVE cannot heal. For this I give thanks.

And so it is.

LOVE

LOVE OPENS THE WAY

"And yet show I unto you a more excellent way."

I Cor. 12:31

Love walks in and opens the door when all else fails. There is no problem on earth that Love cannot heal. Love is the answer to every human need.

Love is the answer to my every need. Love guides me into paths of right-use-ness. Love heals antagonism and dispels hatred. I let Love correct any misunderstandings in my life. I let Love go before me and prepare the way.

I trust my dear ones to omnipresent Love, right where they are. I know that they are safe and divinely protected because Love never faileth.

I am centered in Love. Right where I am is all the Love that there is. Love opens the door to divine right action in my life. Love heals me. Love corrects me and cleanses my heart. Love guides me into perfect paths of everlasting peace. Love is a more excellent way to a perfect experience. The Love of God is my eternal blessing.

And so it is.

LOVE IS THE FULFILLING OF THE LAW

"Owe no man anything, but to love one another; for he that loveth another hath fulfilled the law." Ro. 13:8

The illimitable Love of God expressing in and through me directs me, protects me, and fulfills all of the desires of my life. I know no feeling of separation from any living soul for we are all one as the Love of God works in and through His perfect creation. I send my love out to all of the world and it returns to me from everyone whom I contact. In this way I attune myself with God's wonderful storehouse of Infinite Love and I am blessed, protected, and prospered in everything that I do. I am eternally grateful that I am a divine expression of God's perfect Love and that this Love is the motivating Power of my life.

I love the Lord, my God, with all my heart, and with all my soul, and with all my mind; and my neighbor as myself. And thus God's perfect Law is fulfilled through me.

And so it is.

LOVE

GOD IS LOVING ME NOW

"There shall no evil befall thee." Ps. 91:10

How can I fear if God is ALL IN ALL? God, Infinite Goodness, is everywhere present. Everywhere I go, God is with me, because God is within me and within all of Life.

God is Life. I am enveloped in God's Love each moment of the day and when I go to sleep the Presence of God watches over me. Angels (God's Thoughts) keep me in all ways.

God is loving me through every part of Life. Every little breeze I feel is God caressing me. I am immersed in a sea of Love.

God is loving me through every person that I meet and through every experience. I love Life and Life loves me. Infinite Goodness protects me in all that I do.

And so it is.

MARRIAGE

TREATMENT FOR A HAPPY MARRIAGE

"The fruit of the Spirit is Love." Gal. 5:22

"Marriage to be complete, must first be spiritual. From this inner state of conscious unity in thought, purpose, plan, and action, there comes the outer state corresponding to it, making the outer like the inner, peaceful and harmonious." I share my own inner peace and joy with my marriage partner. My happy marriage reflects the unity within my own mind. That which we give away we keep. I give completely and unreservedly all that I have into my marriage. I am secure in my marriage for the Love of God protects us, guides us, and provides for us abundantly. I am loyal to my marriage partner and my marriage partner is loyal to me. We are One. We joyously serve each other in our family. I bring to my marriage the best that I have. The Love of God is the Essence out of which my perfect marriage is made. God is loving me through my marriage partner. We thank Thee, Father, for this perfect marriage. We trust Thy Love to lead us in wisdom and harmony now and forevermore.

And so it is.

MARRIAGE

GOD IS LOVE

"...Yea, I have loved thee with an everlasting love: therefore with lovingkindness have I drawn thee."

Jer. 31:3

God is Love, God is Infinite and everywhere present in exactly the same degree — Infiniteness. How then can I lack love. I dwell in God and God in me and so I am constantly surrounded, enveloped, immersed and completely integrated in Infinite Love. I can never become separated from this Love. It can never be taken away from me for it is my very Life, my own true Self. Since I know that I have so much Love and can never lose it, I dare to give it away freely. I send it forth to all the world without reservation and it comes back to me as Love in everyone I meet. The Love that I feel in my heart is an irresistible magnet drawing Love to me from every side. As I consciously dwell in Love I am conscious only of Love in my life. I am assured of perfect companionship and I am one with my true love as I am one with God. There is no lack of Love in my life. God is Love and God is loving me through my husband (or wife) and all mankind. I am secure in my love for my security is in God.

And so it is.

MEETING SITUATIONS

"The Lord will perfect that which concerneth me." Ps. 138:8

As we turn to the Spirit of Truth within and ask, "What do I do next? How do I meet this situation?", we find that Love goes before us to prepare the way. Everything that is needed to express Life fully comes into our experience in the right and perfect way

Now, let us bear witness unto the Truth. Let us turn our attention to the Spirit within and there be still and know that there is that within us which knows just who we are and what It has for us to do. Of ourselves, we can do nothing; but the Wisdom within is able to do all things. The Wisdom within knows just how we can best express life each step of the way. It knows what is right for us and guides us into paths of right action. All things are possible to us, through us, when we turn to the Spirit within. Nothing inhibits the forward motion of the Power. We are here to let God live through us in His perfect way.

And so it is.

MENOPAUSE

I WELCOME CHANGE AND BLESS IT FOR GOOD

"There shall no evil happen to the just." Pr. 12:21

When one is going through the menopause, or change of life, many different emotional and bodily changes take place. Our bodies are constantly changing and adjusting. The word "just" means "balance." Life within the mind and body is seeking a new balance. Think to yourself:

I am releasing my mind and my body to perfect balance. New patterns of thought and action are being formed. I am releasing my mind and my body to the perfect unfoldment of life right where I am. New feelings are being established. I love the Spirit of Truth within me and trust it to produce only good in my experience.

I trust the Intelligence within all of Life, within my life and within every cell of my being. I trust God and know that God is doing exactly what is right for me. I am not governed by the appearances of the moment. I am not governed by the feelings of the moment. I am governed by God, the infinite Power and Intelligence within me. The changes that are taking place within me are for my good and I receive them with a smile and a blessing.

And so it is.

OFFICE RELATIONSHIPS

I AM ONE WITH MY FELLOW WORKER

"Not according to our works, but according to his own purpose and grace. II Tim. 1:9

Through our work, we express our faith. "Faith without works is dead." Work is not to be shunned. Work is not lowly nor menial, irrespective of what it may be. It is not a curse, nor is labor a misfortune. One has to be active and creative to enjoy life. The doing of our work must be shared with others. Sometimes others bring into their work their personal problems, thereby causing conflicts and disagreements. These feelings sometimes become contagious and spread among a whole work group. Then is the time to "Golden Key" the situation. This means to turn away from the problems and bring love into play. Think: "I love each and every person employed in this office and I am knowing that love is neutralizing all fear, anxiety, rebellion and hostility. Love fills this office and the minds and hearts of everyone employed here. The Golden Key has been used to unlock the door of love and love flows into every situation in this office. Peace and harmony reign and this office is the center of creative and loving activity."

And so it is.

OFFICE RELATIONSHIPS

GOD IS MY EMPLOYER

"God is love; and he that dwelleth in love dwelleth in God, and God in him. There is no fear in love; but perfect love casteth out fear." I Jn. 4:16, 18

God is my Employer—my work is assured. I am working for God and each day is a blessing. God tells me what to do and gives me the ability to do it in a perfect way. The Infinite Intelligence within me is my ability to do each assignment and perform each duty adequately.

I give forth Love to each one and no longer wonder whether I will please. The Love that I share is generated from an Infinite Source within and calls forth the Love in everyone else, making it impossible for me to give or receive offense.

Perfect Love casts the fear of criticism from my mind. As I rejoice in the Presence of God, I am a blessing to everyone around me. Day by day, Love goes before me and prepares the way. Love looks forth at me from each one's eyes and reaches out a hand to me from everyone I meet. Love protects me and cares for me. I cannot fail when I depend upon God's Wisdom to sustain me. My work will continue for my Employer is Infinite.

And so it is.

OMNIPRESENCE

OMNIPRESENCE   the 139th Psalm

Whither shall I go from Thy Spirit...

Whither can I go from Thy Spirit? Thou art "nearer than breathing, closer than hands or feet," for Thou art my very life, the Intelligence that thinks through me, the Power that works in me, the Substance of me. Thou art all.

Or whither shall I flee from Thy presence?...

Whither can I flee from Thy Presence? Thou art everywhere present. Thy love surrounds and keeps me.

If I ascend up into heaven, Thou art there....

If I ascend up into a high state of consciousness where I abide in the kingdom of heaven within, Thou art there, for in this awareness I am aware of Thee and Thee alone, but....

If I make my bed in hell, behold Thou art there....

Yes, even if I choose to separate myself from Thy omnipresent Love, asleep to Thy blessings, ignorant of Thy Truth, willfully flaunting my little human ego as I struggle with the separateness of personality and false appearances; behold, Thou art there. Right in the midst of my self-imposed misery, Thou art there.

If I take the wings of the morning, and dwell in the uttermost parts of the sea....

Should I go off on some flight of fancy, drifting in a sea of thought to a far country, I find that Thou art there before me. Even the winds and the waves of thought obey Thee.

Even the night shall be light about me. Yea, the darkness hideth not from Thee; but the night shineth as the day; the darkness and the light are both alike to Thee.

Thou art ever present. There is no life but Thy Life. There is no power but Thy Power. Thou art all. I trust in Thee.   And so it is.

OVERWEIGHT

A MEDITATION FOR BALANCED WEIGHT

"It is written, man shall not live by bread alone, but by every word that proceedeth out of the mouth of God."
Matt. 4:4

Spirit is weightless. It moves effortlessly. Spirit is always in balance. There is no heaviness of Spirit, therefore there is no heaviness to take form. Like the rose, all that we need comes to us from Spirit. The food that we eat is the outer symbol of the bread of Life, daily Inspiration that comes as we need it, no more, no less. Divine Guidance comes, as in everything else, from within and is just right for you, acceptable to you and effective for you.

Know daily for yourself: I receive daily food for daily needs, food for my mind and food for my body. There is that within me which knows what is right for me, choosing right thoughts for my mind and right food for my body. Spirit is always in balance and so is its image and likeness. There is no heaviness of Spirit and there is no heaviness in me. This is the Truth and it manifests as my balanced weight.

And so it is.

OVERWEIGHT

THE BODY BEAUTIFUL

"Know ye not that ye are the temple of God, and that the Spirit of God dwelleth in you?" I Cor. 3:16

My body is lithe, supple and flexible; filled with vibrant life. As I cease from burden bearing and consciously release all heaviness of thought, I am freed from heaviness of body. Infinite Intelligence within me selects right thoughts for my mind and right choice of food for my body. Sustained by spiritual food, I no longer crave that which can never satisfy. As I live by inner Guidance I am led to eat only that which I need. I now think of my body as a beautiful instrument of Spirit, the temple of the living God. I live for the moment and I eat for the moment that which I need. God within me knows how to regulate my life and maintain my body in perfect harmonious balance. I need not struggle with diets or make a fetish of weight control. My body is filled with Light, and the Wisdom within me knows how to gauge and control my perfect weight. The Grace of God is my sufficiency in everything.

And so it is.

OVERWORK

I LABOR IN THE VINEYARD WITH JOY

"For he performeth the thing that is appointed for me."
Job 23:14

The burdens that we assume are always of our own making. No one makes us take on responsibilities. Oftentimes this burden of work may belong to another. We take it on because we do not trust the Intelligence within him to do the job as we would do it. At other times when we feel overworked, it is only that there has been poor planning. The yoke is easy and the burden light when we let Divine Intelligence plan and carry out our assignment. Then, everything takes on a proper perspective; bit by bit the pieces fall into place. Life becomes easier and yet is filled with accomplishment.

If you are tempted to feel overworked, stop right where you are and ask yourself a few questions: Are you trying to play God in some situation? Are you putting money and prestige before your spiritual life? Are you letting public opinion direct your endeavor and drive your every moment? Say to the self:

Today, I will put first things first. Today, I will let the Lord build the house; moment by moment I will take my direction from the perfect Power within me that knows what is important for me to do. I accept my challenges as opportunities for accomplishment when I let the Father within plan the work. He performs miracles through me, for me. He works through my hands with precision and ease. All resistance is gone out of me. I agree with my work and my work agrees with me. I bless my work and my work blesses me.

And so it is.

PATIENCE

I CAN AFFORD TO BE PATIENT

"But let patience have her perfect work, that ye may be perfect and entire, wanting nothing." Jas. 1:4

Having faith I can afford to be patient. I really believe that God is taking care of me and my affairs according to His perfect plan for me. Trusting, I can wait. God is working behind the scenes that I may be "perfect and entire, wanting nothing." He who "neither slumbers nor sleeps" watches over me with my best interests at heart. I need not strain at life or attempt to hurry God for He is already pouring out to me more than I can receive. Today I will quietly prepare myself to receive my good, knowing nothing is withheld by my loving Father. No anxious thought disturbs my peace. Trustingly, I await my highest good. And it is done.

And so it is.

PATIENCE

MY TRUST IS IN GOD

"Rest in the Lord and wait patiently for him." Ps. 37:7

Today I will let go and let God, trusting and knowing that my highest good and that of my loved ones is already on its way. In the immortal words of John Burroughs:

> "Serene I fold my hands and wait,
> Nor care for wind, nor tide, nor sea;
> I rave no more 'gainst time or fate,
> For lo, my own shall come to me."

I know that as I keep my eye single, centered on the Wholeness and Perfection of the God Life, nothing but Good can come into my experience. My only desire is to build a solid foundation of spiritual growth, grounded in Truth and Love. I have planted good seeds in the soil of Mind and I trust the Divine Law of Life to bring the harvest at the right and perfect time for me. My faith is in the Great Unseen out of Which that which is seen will appear. My trust is in God. I can afford to be patient.

And so it is.

PEACE OF MIND

I AM PROFOUNDLY UNDISTURBED

"Commit thy way unto the Lord; trust also in him, and he shall bring it to pass." Ps. 37:5

I believe in the Power of Good in my life. There is no power in conditions. There is no power in personalities. I feel nothing done against me. Nothing can disturb me. Nothing in my past life has any power to hurt me. I am making my future by good thinking right now. I commit my way unto the Divine Law of Good in my life. All of my plans, all of my hopes, my friends and my family, I place in His care. I go about my duties with a serene sense of well-being, calm in the assurance that my life and affairs are in Good Hands. I live in the present and trust in the future. I have no regrets. I now accept a wonderful new life for myself, trusting the Infinite Wisdom of God working in and through me to bring it into manifestation. I believe that everything in the Universe is working together for my good. I am undisturbed. I am at peace.

And so it is.

PEACE OF MIND

PEACE OF MIND
(23rd Psalm)

THE LORD IS MY SHEPHERD, I SHALL NOT WANT.
> I am secure and at peace because the Divine Law of Love protects, guides, and leads me.

HE MAKETH ME TO LIE DOWN IN GREEN PASTURES: HE LEADETH ME BESIDE THE STILL WATERS.
> I am centered in Peace. I am calm. The inner awareness of Divine Peace gives me a quiet mind.

HE RESTORETH MY SOUL.
> I am free from guilt or fear and my mind is renewed through God's inner peace. His peace is my peace.

HE LEADETH ME IN THE PATHS OF RIGHTEOUSNESS FOR HIS NAME'S SAKE.
> I trust God's guidance in and through me. His nature is good and all that He does through me is good.

YEA, THOUGH I WALK THROUGH THE VALLEY OF THE SHADOW OF DEATH, I WILL FEAR NO EVIL: FOR THOU ART WITH ME: THY ROD AND THY STAFF THEY COMFORT ME.
> My heart is at peace. God is the only Reality, and He is with me always.

THOU PREPAREST A TABLE BEFORE ME IN THE PRESENCE OF MINE ENEMIES: THOU ANNOINTEST MY HEAD WITH OIL: MY CUP RUNNETH OVER.
> I am at peace with my own thoughts and unified with all of life. I am secure in God's abundance.

SURELY GOODNESS AND MERCY SHALL FOLLOW ME ALL OF THE DAYS OF MY LIFE AND I WILL DWELL IN THE HOUSE OF THE LORD FOR EVER.
> I rest in the continual awareness of the Presence of God within me.

And so it is.

PERFECT PRAYER

THE PERFECT PRAYER

"Our Father which art in heaven, Hallowed be Thy name. Thy kingdom come. Thy will be done, in earth, as it is in heaven. Give us this day our daily bread. And forgive us our debts, as we forgive our debtors. And lead us not into temptation, but deliver us from evil; For thine is the kingdom, and the power, and the glory, forever. Amen. Matt. 6:9-13

Our Father, Feeder, Provider, Protector, First Cause, Divine Principle, Creator and Sustainer of all Good. Thou art everywhere present, all-knowing, all-powerful; Love made manifest as Thy own perfect creation. Wholeness is Thy nature, and we, Thy image and likeness are forever whole as we portray Thee.

In Thy Kingdom there is no sickness, sin, or lack. Thy Kingdom is Love expressing as harmonious right action in every phase of Life. Thy Kingdom is established; as in Thy heaven within, so it is in our earth.

Feed us with Thy word, the Bread of Life.

We know that our sins are forgiven us to the degree that we are able to forgive. Let Thy Love flow through us to all mankind.

In overcoming temptation, we are delivered from evil; There is no power apart from Thee.

Thine is the Kingdom and we, through Love and Law, are given dominion over all the world; but, the Power and the Glory, from first to last, belong to Thee.

Amen.*

*And so it is.

PHYSICAL PERFECTION

I BLESS MY BODY

"Know ye not that ye are the temple of God, and that the Spirit of God dwelleth in you? I Cor. 3:16

I bless my body. It is the "temple of God" — pure Spiritual Substance. Every cell of my body is activated by Divine Intelligence. Every organ in my body is regulated by the Involuntary Life within me, in perfect harmonious action. Each organ in my body is a perfect part of a Perfect Whole — the Perfect Wholeness that is God expressing as me. I bless my body and give thanks for it. It is a faithful servant provided and maintained to house the individualization of God known as myself. I bless my body and release it in perfect confidence to the Father within who "neither slumbers nor sleeps" in His care for me. I trust the Father within to beat my heart, digest my food, circulate my blood and harmonize the entire action of my body. I am the temple of God. The spirit of God dwells within me. I thank Thee, Father, for Thy loving care.

And so it is.

POWER

OF MYSELF I CAN DO NOTHING

"I can of mine own self do nothing...the Father that dwelleth in me, he doeth the works." Jn. 5:30, Jn. 14:10

These beautiful, mystical words of Jesus contain the secret of his success in living the Christ and demonstrating the mighty Power of the Creative Source of all Life, which he called "the Father within." Perhaps if we really understood them, we, too, could do the things he promised we could do..."And even greater things shall ye do because I go unto the Father." If we follow his example and "go unto the Father," the Source of all Power which is to be found right at the center of our own being, we, too, can heal the sick, cast out demons, and do other mighty works in His name, which means, according to the divine nature which is ours. Know for the self:

Of myself, I can do nothing, the Wisdom within, It doeth the works. Of my little self, I am completely inadequate, but as I unify with the mighty Power within me and let this Power express through me into life, all Power is given unto me in heaven (within) and earth (without). With Thee, all things are possible.

And so it is.

PRACTICING THE PRESENCE

I WALK WITH GOD

"And Enoch walked with God." Gen. 5:24

Today, like Enoch, I will walk with God. I feel His warm, loving presence welling up within me and shining all around me like sunshine on a spring morning. I let God's Infinite Wisdom go before me and be my Guide in everything that I do. If there is some situation in my life that does not seem clear to me, I will take no anxious thought. I "trust in the Lord and wait patiently for Him" for to Him the answers are already known. I do not fret for I know that His ways are ways of peace. I walk with God and am not afraid. Right where I am is all of the Intelligence I will ever need, and it is revealed through me as divine Inspiration. These perfect ideas are made manifest to me as spiritual Substance which takes form as whatever I need. As I walk with God I am perfectly cared for each step of the way. His love surrounds me. How can I fear? The journey is pleasant. I rejoice each step of the way.

And so it is.

PRACTICING THE PRESENCE

GOD IS ALWAYS AVAILABLE TO ME

"If I ascend up into heaven, thou art there: if I make my bed in hell, behold, thou art there." Ps. 139:8

In my foolishness, I thought that I had become separated from the Goodness of God within me. Now I know that this could not be possible. I think, therefore I am part of the Infinite Mind. I live, therefore I am part of the Infinite Life of God. Even my false, negative thinking cannot separate me from the Truth of my own being. Everywhere I go, "thou art there." God is always available to me as Infinite Goodness, that Love that will not let me go.

Today I accept more of the Presence of God in my thinking, knowing that the measure of Goodness I can accept in my inner experience becomes the measure of Goodness outpictured in my outer experience.

God is all in all, everywhere present. I can never be separated from God for a single instant. I am a divine, perfect, spiritual being, uncontaminated by lack, sickness or mental confusion. I am an idea in the Mind of God and God is thinking me into expression right now — *"thoughts of peace and not of evil, to give me an expected end." My awareness of the Presence of God in my mind and heart is my answer to every seeming problem. In the valleys and on the mountain tops, Thou art there.

And so it is.

*Jer. 29:11

PRAYING FOR OTHERS

NO PRAYER IS EVER WASTED

"God was in Christ, reconciling the world unto himself, not imputing their trespasses unto them; and hath committed unto us the word of reconciliation." II Cor. 5:19

At some time or other, each one of us faces the task of trying to help someone who seems buried beneath the hard shell of materiality, impossible to reach. Our hearts ache for this dear one who trusts neither God nor man, seeming to live in a world of enemies.

It is then that we must stand fast in affirming the Christ within.

I know that this person has never for one instant been separated from God. His lonely sense of separation is only an illusion. He is, in Truth, the son of the living God, and the Infinite Power of God lives through him, his divine potential. Nothing can keep him from the reality of his true being. I know not at which moment his awakening will come. The battle is not mine, but the Lord's. God is in this world as the Christ within him, reconciling the world unto himself. The Spirit of Truth within him reveals to him all that he needs to know.

And so it is.

PRAYING FOR OTHERS

A TREATMENT FOR ANOTHER

"Mark the perfect man, and behold the upright; for the end of that man is peace." Ps. 37:37

I am no longer anxious about my loved one for I behold him healed. My mistake has been in looking at the problem. I now turn my attention completely to God and see His creation perfect. There is not God *and* man, but God *as* man, the glory Jesus knew before the world began.

I do not have to struggle to change another; my role is to behold the perfection of God's original creation which can never be changed. The healing takes place in my mind. I do not have to convince another or change anyone. Since we are one in Mind, I need only reveal to myself the Truth that already exists. I see the perfect man and "the end of that man is peace".

In Mind, the past is wiped away and a glorious future appears in the visible world. The wilderness along the way begins to blossom. My treatment for another becomes a joy instead of a labor as I cease to struggle with conditions and turn my attention to First Cause which is always whole and complete. The responsibility is with God and God never fails. I rest in His Love. I release my loved one to Him, with thanksgiving, and confidently accept the healing.

And so it is.

PRESSURE

GOD NEVER HURRIES

"He that believeth shall not make haste." Isa. 28:16

There is only one time. That time is now.

There is no wrong time. I am always in the right place doing the right thing at the right perfect time.

There is no waste time. I am using my time wisely and intelligently.

There is no lack of time. I am in an eternal experience.

There are no wasted years. Everything that has transpired in my life brings me to this moment of divine unfoldment and understanding.

There is no time of trouble. Now is the time of salvation and I am saved by the Love and Power of God.

I have no regrets for the past. I live this moment fully and in the Joy of God.

Time was made for man, not man for time. Time is Infinite — Eternal in the heavens. Now is all the time there is. This is the only moment I can live. I am relaxed and peaceful in it. God never hurries. God's time is my time. It is always sufficient for my needs. I use it in an orderly manner.

And so it is.

PRIDE GOES OUT WHEN LOVE COMES IN

"Pride goeth before destruction." Pr. 16:18

Pride sneaks in like the soldiers hidden in the Trojan horse. It seems so natural to want things and then be proud of them; to desire accomplishment and then be proud of it; to gain good companions and then be proud of them; to be proud of one's family and one's success. But, beware. Pride can be the most powerful enemy that we entertain in our mental household; for with pride comes a sense of protecting what we have lest it be taken from us, and still more devastating, a deep concern over how we might appear in the opinion of others. Pride leaves us vulnerable to every barbed remark, to every passing look, and to our own inaccurate human judgment.

We must ask ourselves this: Are we proud of ourselves, or are we glorifying God? Is our pride based on the prayer of the Pharisee, "I thank thee, God, that I am not like the rest of men," or is it based on the certainty that "all things come of thee"?

Only the feelings can be hurt. Only the ego is bruised. Without God we are helpless and hopeless, but the Father within is never discouraged by man's opinion. As we let God live through us we discover we have nothing to protect. The battle is not ours but the Lord's.

Know for yourself:

I am now accepting my good as the gift of God. With God all things are possible. Every challenge that comes into my life is an opportunity to express God; every accomplishment is God expressing through me; every friend is God sharing with me; every member of my family is God unified with me; my every success is God's order living through me. My word is God's word at my point of use. I rejoice that I am a son of God. I recognize this sonship in every man I meet.

And so it is.

PROSPERITY

I ENJOY PROSPEROUS LIVING

"They shall prosper that love Thee." Ps. 122:6

I am prosperity. The substance of wealth is within me. I seek first the kingdom of divine Good within and its right use, knowing that all that I need is added unto me.

I give freely and receive joyfully out of a sense of Abundance. I dare to give from an Infinite Source. I receive my good gladly, allowing others the joy of giving. My Abundance is of God. There is no power in lack. I use God's gifts wisely and joyfully. I accept my good with confidence. I am worthy of being a son of God and all that the Father hath is mine. I put God first in my life.

I give the first fruits to God — a tenth of all that I receive. As I tithe I prosper. In the spirit that I give to God, God gives to me. I give freely and joyfully out of a grateful heart. I am prospered in all that I do.

And so it is.

PROSPERITY

GOD PROSPERS THROUGH ME

"Now unto him that is able to do exceeding abundantly above all that we ask or think, according to the power that worketh in us..." Eph. 3:20

God **P**roves through me by opening the windows of heaven and pouring out such a blessing that there is not room enough to receive it.

God **R**eaps through me a harvest of good things, the fullness of Life outpictured in my experience.

God **O**perates through me, to give me the ability and skill to succeed in all that I undertake.

God **S**erves through me freely, giving forth the best that is in me and I am blessed a hundredfold.

God **P**roduces through me with ease and assurance all that I need for a successful and abundant life.

God **E**xpresses through me a wealth of ideas which become my abundant supply.

God **R**eceives through me His perfect Life ever expanding into endless expression "and no good thing will He withhold".

And so it is.

PROSPERITY

I THINK PROSPERITY

"So shall my word be that goeth forth out of my mouth ...it shall prosper in the thing whereto I send it."

Isa. 55:11

My word for good renders successful everything I undertake. I expect success and I find success. My feeling of inner Wealth neutralizes any suggestion of lack on the outside. The Wholeness of God within is my Wealth. God's Abundance is my abundance. It flows through my mind into manifestation. God gives me ideas and clothes them with all that is needed to bring them into perfect form. The moment I cease to struggle with outside conditions and turn to the Infinite Source within, the floodgates are opened and good is poured forth into my experience.

I am employed by God who rewards my services with lavish praise and generous remuneration. I think prosperity. I speak prosperity. I am prosperity. My every act produces prosperity. I dare to give as freely as I receive, knowing that I cannot outgive God. I think prosperity and I demonstrate prosperity to the glory of God who lives through me. And for this I am most grateful.

And so it is.

PROTECTION

GOD IS MY PROTECTION WHEREVER I GO

"He that dwelleth in the secret place of the most High shall abide under the shadow of the Almighty." Ps. 91:1

God is my security, His Truth my shield and buckler. I am secure in the knowledge that although a thousand shall fall at my side and ten thousand at my right hand, it shall not come nigh me. His angel thoughts have taken charge of me to keep me in all my ways. Because I know that He is my refuge and my fortress, I have nothing to fear. He cares for me always.

In the secret place of the most High, in that blessed Silence, I hear my God Self speak to me, "Be still and know that I am God...I will not leave thee nor forsake thee...whithersoever thou goest, I will go with thee... when thou passest through the waters, I will be with thee...I will go before thee and make the crooked places straight...there shall no evil befall thee, neither shall any plague come nigh thy dwelling."

God is my protection wherever I go. I am immersed in His Love as the fish is immersed in the sea. I feel It all about me, a warm, loving Presence. I am clothed in an armor of love and nothing can by any means hurt me. For this I give thanks.

And so it is.

RELAXATION

HOW TO RELAX

I am relaxed. Every muscle, every cell, every atom of my body is relaxed. I am letting go and letting God direct and maintain my life and affairs. I am resting on the Everlasting Arms. I am taking dominion and giving the following orders to my body:

My toes are relaxed (flex the toes, tense them, turn them up toward the head and then consciously release and relax them.)

My feet are relaxed (tense the feet and then consciously relax them.)

My ankles are relaxed (tense the ankles and then consciously relax them.)

My calves are relaxed (tense the calves and then consciously relax them.)

My knees are relaxed (tense the knees and then consciously relax them.)

My thighs are relaxed (tense the thighs and then consciously relax them.)

My hips are relaxed (tense the hips and then consciously relax them.)

My fingers are relaxed (tense the fingers and then consciously relax them.)

My hands are relaxed (tense the hands and then consciously relax them.)

My arms are relaxed (tense the arms and then consciously relax them.)

My diaphragm is relaxed (tense the diaphragm and then consciously relax it.)

Now I am letting my shoulders relax, letting go of any burden I have been carrying. I am relaxing my neck muscles (tense them then relax them). I am relaxed. My scalp is relaxed...my head is relaxed...my brain is relaxed...my mind is relaxed...my eyes are relaxed... my face is relaxed (let expression go limp)...my whole body is relaxed. Now in this relaxed state, I surrender myself to the Perfect Power within me. I realize that all of life continues without my doing anything about it...I AM LETTING GO AND LETTING GOD!

And so it is.

RELAXATION

I AM RELAXED

"Come unto me all ye that labour and are heavy laden, and I will give you rest." Matt. 11:28

I am completely, perfectly and wholly relaxed. I am letting go right now of every muscle, every nerve, every bone, every tissue in my body. I rest in the knowledge that there is within me an Intelligence which knows how to function my body perfectly, which knows how to function my affairs perfectly, which knows how to function my life perfectly. I let the Intelligence within me tell me what to do and how to do it. I move easily through life, doing the right thing at exactly the right time. I am free from any irritation. I am in perfect harmony with life. Nothing irritates me. No person annoys me. I do not condemn myself. I have no anxiety for the future. I surrender my every action; my every demand; my every fear, worry, anxiety, and burden to God within me whom I worship and adore. I trust God to care for me knowing that divine right action is operating in all of my affairs. I am completely relaxed in God.

And so it is.

RELEASE OF LOVED ONES

I RELEASE MY LOVED ONES TO GOD

"The law of the Lord is perfect, converting the soul."
Ps. 19:7

I release my loved ones to God. Only the perfect Law can understand the lives of others. What seems to be evil to me may be good in the making, the way that another will receive his growth and his blessing. I release each one to his perfect unfoldment, knowing that the Infinite Intelligence within him knows just how to bring his life and affairs into balance. We are all in an eternal experience. The Law works always for good but who can say just how it shall act.

I refuse to be irritated. To become embroiled in another's confusion hurts me and helps him not at all. To sorrow for another's suffering puts me where he is in consciousness and there I cannot help him. To see evil is to turn from God.

I rejoice that I am able to help by keeping my attention focused on God. God (Good) is all that there is. The false appearances are but a dream, a false concept. I cease to be meddlesome and become an instrument of healing as I behold in my loved ones the activity of God.

And so it is.

RELEASE OF OTHERS

I BECOME FREE BY FREEING OTHERS

"Whatsoever thou shalt bind on earth shall be bound in heaven: and whatsoever thou shalt loose on earth shall be loosed in heaven." Matt. 16:19

The Kingdom of Heaven is at hand. I am free to experience it the moment I free others. I serve my fellow man by releasing him to his own highest good. I release the past knowing that Principle is not bound by precedent. No condition of the past has power over me. I release my children, freeing them to grow and express in their own individual ways. I release my friends from any confining thoughts I may have had about them.

Since the creative word of life is constantly recreating the world, I know that yesterday's failure is today's success. Everywhere I look I see the Life of God made manifest. I see the Wholeness of God in every physical body and this Wholeness is reflected in me. I feel the Love of God in every human heart and according to the Law of Life, this is the Love I am able to receive in my life. I become free by freeing others, and for this I am most grateful.

And so it is.

RELEASE OF PROBLEM

I RELEASE MY PROBLEM IN PERFECT TRUST

"Because the creature itself also shall be delivered from the bondage of corruption into the glorious liberty of the children of God." Ro. 8:21

I release my problem to God in perfect trust. "The government is upon His shoulder." His infinite wisdom knows the answer that my finite mind cannot perceive. "Thy will be done" is a joyous release to my futile struggling and an open door to unlimited good. The Father knows the perfect way to bring peace and right action into the situation. He transforms into victory. Wondrous are His ways and past all finding out.

Every moment that I have spent in the past fretting over "evil-doers" is a moment I have not shared with God. I now have no time for fussing, complaining or railing. I must be about my Father's business — giving in love to all mankind.

I now forgive all those who have hurt me. I bless them in their onward journey. I trust God to protect me and all those whom I love. I face the future with glad assurance. Only Good can manifest to the one who loves. I release my problem to God in perfect trust.

And so it is.

RELEASE TO GOD

GOD KNOWS HOW

"But Jesus beheld them, and said unto them, With men this is impossible; but with God all things are possible."
Matt. 19:26

God knows how to become blossoms and fruit on the tree. I don't, but God knows how.

God knows how to keep the stars and planets secure in their courses, to regulate the tides and seasons in a perfect plan.

God knows how to produce unlimited power out of the rocks of the earth as oil and atomic power; and out of the heavens as electricity and solar power. No man can fathom God's work. Only the Infinite understands.

God knows how to join two cells and produce a beautiful little body complete to the last detail. No man can reproduce Life; but, God creates and maintains His creation according to a plan so magnificent that it is beyond the vision of man to behold the glory of it. God knows how to turn food into blood and flesh and bones, how to constantly create new body cells and supply the muscles with strength. We know that it happens but we cannot understand this miracle.

I now release all my problems to Him who knows how to solve them and say with Jesus, "of myself I can do nothing, the Father within me doeth the works". Oh, how beautifully He does them. I surrender my life completely to God, the only Power and the only Presence.

And so it is.

RENTAL OF PROPERTY

THE PERFECT TENANT IS DRAWN TO ME

"But as it is written, Eye hath not seen, nor ear heard, neither have entered into the heart of man, the things which God hath prepared for them that love him."

I Cor. 2:9

The rental of this property does not depend upon luck or chance. Having lovingly provided for my new tenant, I know that he will be drawn to the home which has been prepared for him. I know that there is a right and perfect tenant for my property, a person who will love it, care for it, beautify it, and pay his rent promptly and gladly. In the one Mind this tenant is known and even now is being guided to my house. God has ways of drawing together those who belong together. This action takes place in Mind.

I see myself renting my property. As I walk through the empty rooms I see them filled with loving, happy people. I see the new tenants exclaiming over this property, telling me over and over that it is just what they have been seeking. It is accomplished in Mind. I accept the rent from happy tenants. We are both pleased. All is well. With calm expectancy of good, I release my property into the hands of God. The outer experience is certain to follow at the right and perfect time. I rest in the awareness of my certain good. I am most grateful.

And so it is.

RESENTMENT

LOVE HEALS ME OF ALL RESENTMENT

"Great peace have they which love thy law: and nothing shall offend them." Ps. 119:165

Nothing offends me for I am grounded in Love. God is my protection, I shall not fear. My conscious awareness of Love is a protection to myself and those who know me.

Love is the only power. Only Love goes from me and only Love returns to me. There is nothing to fear. Love heals antagonism. Love nullifies resentment. Love guards and protects. I dwell peacefully in Love, knowing constant protection. Love welds me together with all mankind. Never again need I feel lonely or afraid. Divine Love at the center of my being is my freedom from sin and mistake. Since Love surrounds me at all times, there is nothing to resent.

Infinite Father, Eternal Mother, perfect Love at the center of my being, I trust in Thee. Turning from the confused evidence of the senses, I find my security within and trust it always.

And so it is.

RESISTANCE TO TAXES

I AGREE WITH LIFE

"Be not overcome of evil, but overcome evil with good."
Ro. 12:21

Jesus, the greatest teacher of them all, saw the need to overcome resistance to any part of life, even to the paying of taxes. "Render unto Caesar," he said, "the things which are Caesar's and unto God the things that are God's." He, himself, did not resist the payment of taxes but demonstrated how one might produce the tax money easily. If we really believe that God is all in all, then we must accept God as being in every part of life. If God, infinite Goodness, is the only Cause and Creator, we must be willing to trust God in every part of life. There is no segment of life that is separated out of the Kingdom of God. Treat daily to know:

God is loving me now. God is loving me through every part of Life. God is loving me through every person, every situation, every circumstance in life. God is loving me through my business. God is loving me through the stock market. It is the Father's good pleasure to give me the Kingdom. Therefore I am given ideas to prosper me.

Whenever I pay taxes I pay with a feeling of giving to God's work, made possible through taxes; such as, schools, parks, beauty and protection. Taking my attention from human graft and greed, I mentally assign my tax money to constructive use. I give it freely because I trust divine Intelligence to work out the problems of government and spend my money wisely.

I am God's steward. I have plenty and to spare. I receive from Abundance and give to Abundance. The Source of my supply is Infinite.

And so it is.

RIGHT ACTION

HE SHALL BRING IT TO PASS

"Commit thy way unto the Lord; trust also in him; and he shall bring it to pass." Ps. 37:5

I commit my way unto the divine Law of Life and experience perfect right action in my life and affairs. I plant good thoughts in Mind and patiently await good results, knowing that the Law will always respond to me at the right and perfect time. The Lord (divine Law) will perfect all that concerns me.

The Will of God for me is always for my highest good, not as a stern disciplinary action, but as a joyous unfolding of Love. I do not need to beg the indulgence of my heavenly Father. His gifts are so lavish and so freely given that they almost overwhelm me. He asks only that I accept His Love and give it back as trust and confidence. He asks only that I cease to struggle with outer conditions and look to Him for all my needs fulfilled. My cup runneth over. God is able to create for me an abundance of every good thing, far more than I can ever conceive of. The Love that I hold in my secret heart becomes manifest in a tangible way for all the world to see. The Law is good. I can never say "thank you" enough.

And so it is.

RESPONSIBILITY

I AM RESPONSIBLE ONLY TO GOD

"Call upon me in the day of trouble: I will deliver thee, and thou shalt glorify me." Ps. 50:15

I realize that the tendency to think that we should change others, heal others, and make the world conform to our beliefs is erroneous and will produce a feeling of burden and defeat.

How can I expect God to respond to me when I try to take over His work? I have learned that God can do all things and that nothing is impossible to Him. Since this is so, I cast my burden on Him.

I now rely completely, wholly and unconditionally upon God. He is responsible and does respond to my seeking, asking, and knocking. How wonderful to know that God does the work that fulfills my every need, desire and request.

I know the one asking for help is healed — God heals him.

I know the task is done — God does it.

I know the work is completed — God completes it.

I know that perfect peace now is — God establishes it.

I know that God is my Spirit, my Life, my All-in-All.

And so it is.

RESPONSIBILITY

THE BATTLE IS NOT MINE, BUT GOD'S

"Thus saith the Lord unto you, Be not afraid nor dismayed by reason of this great multitude; for the battle is not yours, but God's." II Chron. 20:15

When I am tempted to feel a great responsibility, either for myself or another, I step aside a little bit and say, "The battle is not mine but God's." Releasing all responsibility to God, the only Power, I realize that I shall not need to fight in this battle. My part is to establish myself in Truth and see the salvation of the Lord with me. Like Jehoshaphat of old, I praise the Lord and the "enemies" fall to the earth. Where there were problems, now there are answers. Antagonism is transformed into loving cooperation. All things work together for good when I stop to praise God. Standing firmly on the rock of Truth, I see that that which seemed to come against me was but a figment of my imagination. The divine Law of Life has transformed each situation into the likeness of Love. My responsibility is my response-ability to God. The battle is not mine but God's. Father, I release everything and everyone into Thy care. Resting in Thy Love I behold the victory of Love.

And so it is.

SALE OF PROPERTY

I RECEIVE MY GOOD

"A man can receive nothing, except it be given him from heaven." Jn. 3:27

That which we can accept in the heaven within is bound to become our experience. The question is: what have we been accepting? Have we felt that we had a piece of property that was hard to sell? Have we thought of it as a worthless investment? Have we secretly thought that we were asking too much for it? If we are honest with the Law of Life, the Law will be honest with us. Love the property, bless the property, bless the person who is to be the new owner. It only takes one and he will be drawn to you from somewhere.

Know for the self: In heaven within, that divine awareness of being one with God, I accept my good and it appears in my world as a visible manifestation.

The sale of this property is already accomplished in the one Mind. There is a right and perfect person who will enjoy this property. I now accept the culmination of this sale in such a way that it will bless all concerned. In the one Mind I mentally hand the property over to the new owner and receive from him the right remuneration in exchange. His good is my good. I accept only that which is fair to both of us. Divine Justice directs this sale and all are blessed in its transaction. For this I give thanks.

And so it is.

SECURITY

MY SECURITY IS IN GOD

"Thou wilt keep him in perfect peace, whose mind is stayed on Thee; because he trusteth in Thee." Isa. 26:3

God is my perfect life. In Spirit I live and move and have my being. God is in me and in all of Life. The same God Who holds the stars in their courses and maintains the whole Universe in perfect balance keeps me in perfect balance now. Because I trust infinite Power continuously, I know perfect peace at all times. I dwell in the secret place of the most High and His angel thoughts keep me in all my ways. My security is in God. My every need is met before it has time to become a lack in my life. I commit my way unto the Lord and my body and my circumstances are maintained in perfect balance with the harmonious whole of Life. The events in my life are perfectly synchronized in the beautiful symphony of spiritual life. Order is the first rule of heaven. God's heaven within becomes my balanced world. This is the peace that passes all understanding. I am content.

And so it is.

SELF REALIZATION

I AM A SON OF GOD

"Wherefore thou art no more a servant, but a son; and if a son, then an heir of God through Christ." Gal. 4:7

God is Life, the One Infinite Source of all Life, dynamic, inexhaustible, continuously creating Itself into expression. God is infinite Mind, all-Knowing, all-Wise, eternal Principle of never-failing Truth, that Light that lighteth every man. God is Love, divine, perfect, compassionate, forgiving, everlasting, omnipresent Goodness, constantly pouring Itself out through Its entire creation. God is Power, almighty Power, omnipotent Strength which can never fail or become depleted, and to which nothing is impossible.

As I recognize myself as the son of God, the image and likeness of the one perfect God, one with the Father, my infinite Source, I become heir to the Kingdom for I lay claim to all of the attributes of God. As the son of an ever-loving Father, I can never be limited or lacking in any way. As I claim my divine sonship, I dwell in the Father's house, (consciousness of the presence of God right where I am) and all that the Father hath is mine. How thankful I am that it is so!

And so it is.

SELF REALIZATION

I AM THE EXPRESSION OF GOD

"I am that I am." Ex. 3:14

I am (insert own name here) a divine, perfect, spiritual being. I am the expression of God within me. I live in a mental world. I am the expression of the omnipotent, all-knowing Power within me. It loves me with an everlasting Love. It knows all that I need to know. It guides me in perfect ways. It wants me to be happy always. The Power expressing through me does all things easily, beautifully, joyously; for It is the Christ, the son of the living God. All sense of limitation and failure slip away as I behold myself as the unique and wonderful individualization of Spirit that I am.

I (insert own name here) am living God's Life in a wonderful way. I am a divine, perfect, spiritual being. My world outpictures my awareness of God.

And so it is.

SELF REALIZATION

CHRIST IS BORN IN ME

Today, the Christ is born in me.

The Christ in me is Wholeness — my perfect Health.
The Christ in me is Wealth — it becomes all that I need.
The Christ in me is Love reflected back to me from every side.
The Christ in me is Right Action in all of my affairs.
The Christ in me is Peace that stills the troubled waters.
The Christ in me is Joy outpicturing as happiness in my life.
The Christ in me is Goodness so satisfying I need make no mistakes.
The Christ in me is Strength through which I can do all things.
The Christ in me is Power to which all things are possible.
The Christ in me is the Christ in YOU and we are ONE.
The Christ in me is God in Action expressed as me.
The Christ in me is THE BELOVED SON IN WHOM HE IS WELL PLEASED.

The Christ is born in me today.

And so it is.

SKIN IRRITATION

I AM SENSITIVE ONLY TO GOD

"Let the beauty of the Lord, our God, be upon us."
Ps. 90:17

My skin is the visible outer layer of the harmonious body temple. It is sensitive only to God. Nothing from without can irritate it. There is no break in the rhythmic harmony of Life. Any sense of irritation, frustration, or resentment in me is now healed by Love. There is no power in conditions, situations or personalities. Nothing can irritate me unless I let it and I respond only to Good. Life circulates freely through the pores of my skin. Spirit in everchanging form is constantly renewing the cells of my body. My skin out-pictures the smooth, unblemished consciousness of God-centered thinking. There is no hidden irritation in my life. My environment is calm, serene and well ordered, and my skin smoothly portrays my harmonious adjustment to life. Spirit shines through me in uninterrupted perfection. I am sensitive only to God and my skin glows with this inner Beauty.

And so it is.

STRENGTH

THE WILL OF GOD IN ME IS STRENGTH

"I can do all things through Christ which strengtheneth me." Phil. 4:13

The will of God in me is strength, not weakness. As I turn trustingly to the Father within, I am given the Guidance I need. Realizing that "of myself I can do nothing", I cease my futile, limited strivings, and confidently step out on faith in the omnipotent Power that is extended to me. The will of God in me is for my highest good, divine right action in my life and affairs. There is no power in conditions, situations, or personalities. All Power belongs to God, almighty God within me. I am through with limited thinking resulting in weakness and futility. I let the perfect will of God be done in me that the almighty Power of God may be expressed in me. The will of God in me is strength, not weakness. "I can do all things through Christ which strengtheneth me."

And so it is.

I SUCCEED TO THE GLORY OF GOD

"The earth is the Lord's and the fulness thereof; the world and they that dwell therein." Ps. 24:1

We draw our experience out of the Infinite. There is no great or small as far as God is concerned; there is only the fulness thereof. If we can accept our good, God is willing. The measure that we hold up to Life determines our success. As we expand our thinking, we expand our experience. Life is willing to give us more than we can ever imagine.

Infinite Intelligence provides the ideas and each idea contains right within it all that it needs to bring it into manifestation. Just as the seed contains within it the roots, the stalk, the blossom, and the fruit; so does the embryonic idea contain the ways and means of certain success.

The earth is the Lord's and the fulness thereof. There is no scrimping in the fulness thereof. In the infinite Mind there is enough and to spare, plenty of ideas, plenty of customers, plenty of the symbol known to us as money. The only requirement is that we receive it first in consciousness. Nothing is withheld when we look to consciousness for our supply. God accomplishes through us. Our success is God's success. God does not know failure. How, then, can we?

Know for the self: I am filled with the fulness of God. That which I need is within me now. Ideas come to me; and these ideas bear fruit. I give and receive from an infinite Source. I succeed to the glory of God.

And so it is

SUPPLY

THE GRACE OF GOD IS MY SUFFICIENCY IN EVERYTHING

"But my God shall supply all your need." Phil. 4:19

The Grace of God, the illimitable Love of God expressed in and through all of Life, is my sufficiency in everything! I know that my every need is gloriously met through this knowledge. I have only to turn, believing, to the loving Father within, to have every need met.

Therefore, I will not fret, no matter what the situation seems to be. I will cease all anxiety and trust in the divine Law of my being, knowing that It is like a loving father who desires only good for his children. The will of God for me is for health, wholeness, and prosperity even greater than I can imagine. I trust the almighty Power working within me and all of life to bring these blessings into my experience easily and harmoniously. As I take the necessary human footsteps, trusting "the still small voice within" to guide me aright, the Grace of God is my sufficiency in everything.

And so it is.

THANKSGIVING

IT IS GOOD TO GIVE THANKS

"Giving thanks unto the Father, which hath made us meet to be partakers of the inheritance of the saints in light." Col. 1:12

Father, I thank Thee:
- that Thou hearest me always.
- that no word from Thee is void of Power.
- that Thou dost confirm Thy word with signs following.
- that Thou hast hid these things from the wise and prudent and hast revealed them unto babes.
- that all Power in heaven (within) and earth (without) is given me of the Father.
- that the former things are passed away. In Christ I am a new creation.
- that we are all one in Thee.
- that I can do all things through Christ.
- that Thy grace is my sufficiency in everything.
- that of myself I can do nothing, but through Thee all things are possible.
- that by remaining true to Thy perfect Life within, I can at all times experience peace of mind, guidance, and divine right action in all that I do.

And so it is.

TROUBLESOME PEOPLE

THERE ARE NO TROUBLESOME PEOPLE

"Blessed are the peacemakers: for they shall be called the children of God." Matt. 5:9

Everything that I do today will be centered in the idea of peace. Everywhere I go I take my peace with me. Nothing from without can disturb me. Where there appears to be "troubled waters", I say, "Peace be still". Where there is dissension and discord, I recognize the oneness of Life. Where there is bitterness and resentment, I sow Love. Wherever I go, I silently establish unity. I no longer seek to have my own way, but let the perfect will of God be done. The Christ in me is one with the Christ in all. As I calmly and serenely unify with the Infinite Love of God within me, everything in my world becomes harmonious. I resist no one and no one resists me. I love everyone. There are no troublesome people in my life. The peace of God radiates from me to everyone I meet. I am a peacemaker. I dwell in the kingdom of harmony and joy. I bring love and peace wherever I go.

And so it is.

TRUSTING IN GOD

MY SURE DEFENSE

"Whoso putteth his trust in the Lord shall be safe."
Pr. 29:25

I know that to be disturbed about one's life and affairs, even for an instant, is not to trust God. I know that God is taking care of me. I trust His loving care in every thing that I do. If things seem to go wrong, I am not disturbed. My life and affairs may be seeking a balance, but my highest good is sure to come out of the action. I love the Divine Law of Life and trust It in every part of my life. Nothing can offend me. If someone speaks harshly to me or seeks to take advantage of me it does not disturb me. My peace is assured; my life is untroubled for I trust in the Law. I dwell in a circle of Love and nothing but love can enter that circle. My awareness of the Presence of God in my life is my sure defense against all seeming evil. In the clear, bright light of Truth there is no darkness or confusion. Nothing troubles me. I do not give or receive offense. Love is the Law of my life. Great peace is mine.

And so it is.

UNDERSTANDING GOD

GOD IS ALL IN ALL

"Be ye therefore perfect, even as your Father which is in heaven is perfect." Matt. 5:48

God in me is perfect Life.

God is Omnipotence — All-Power in me.

God is Wisdom — Infinite Intelligence for me to use.

God is Love — All that I give forth comes back to me.

God is Peace — In my heart and reaching into every part of my life.

God's Right-use-ness guarantees right Action in all of my affairs.

God's Abundance becomes my bountiful supply.

God is Omnipresent — Wherever I am God is!

God knows no problems — God is Perfection.

And so it is.

I TAKE MY PEACE WITH ME

"Blessed are the peacemakers for theirs is the kingdom of heaven." Matt. 5:9

Everything that I do today will be centered in the idea of peace. Everywhere I go I take my peace with me. Nothing from without can distrub me. Where there appears to be "troubled waters" I say "Peace be still." Where there is dissention and discord I recognize the Oneness of all of Life. Where there is bittterness and resentment I sow Love. Wherever I go I silently establish unity. I no longer seek to have my own way, but to let the perfect will of God be done. The Christ in me is one with the Christ in all. As I calmly and serenely become unified with the infinite Love of God within me, everything in my world becomes harmonious. I resist no one and no one resists me. I love everyone and there are no troublesome people in my life. The peace of God radiates from me to everyone that I meet. I am a peacemaker. I dwell in the kingdom of harmony and joy right now. I bring love and peace wherever I go.

And so it is.

VACATION

A VACATION MEDITATION

"Be strong and of a good courage; be not afraid, neither be thou dismayed: for the Lord thy God is with thee whithersoever thou goest." Josh. 1:9

I am not alone. Wherever I am — God is. Wherever I go, I go with God. Should travelling be in order, I have no fear. His Love goes before me and prepares the way. Right lodging and perfect meals await me as I need them. I dedicate both my car and the trip to God. His hand is on the wheel and His Wisdom assures the smooth operation of the car. His Love reaches out to help me through everyone I meet. Each mile of the way is a glorious adventure in the Practice of the Presence of God. How can I feel lonely or apprehensive with His promise singing in my heart — "Whithersoever thou goest I will go with thee. I will not leave thee or forsake thee." I am not alone. The Spirit of God goes with me to companion and protect me each moment of the day. I am never away from home when I dwell in the house of the Lord.

And so it is.

WHEN THINGS GO WRONG

WHEN THINGS GO WRONG

"Trust in the Lord with all thine heart; and lean not unto thine own understanding. In all thy ways acknowledge him, and he shall direct thy paths." Proverbs 3:5

Things may seem to go wrong. Our plans may change, but nothing has changed with God; nothing has gone wrong with the Spirit within us, nothing can happen to the Power of God that is right where we are. It makes no difference what may seem to happen, what may be man's opinion, there is only one Power, the Power of God, and It is the same yesterday, today, and forever. Nothing can interfere with the perfect right action of God Almighty within us. When we stand firm in this knowing, conditions right themselves and the very things that seemed to go wrong turn out to be blessings in disguise. When things seem to go wrong it is only the challenge, the challenge to trust in the Power of God within us, around us, everywhere present.

Trust in the divine Law of Life with all your heart, your whole feeling nature; trust in the Law of infinite Goodness and know that it will direct your path as you move through life from glory to glory, from one good experience to another. As we accept nothing but good, all things work together for good to them that love good.

And so it is.

WISDOM

GOD SPEAKS THROUGH ME

"For it is not ye that speak, but the spirit of your Father that speaketh in you." Matt. 10:20

The Spirit of God, Universal Truth, tells me this day and every day all that I need to know, all that I need to say. The infinite Intelligence within me places the inspiration in my heart and the words in my mouth. As I turn within for my Guidance, divine Wisdom speaks through me easily and quietly. The thoughts that come to my mind are loving, harmonious, and creative, according to the nature of God. All stress and strain goes out of my voice for I feel the Wisdom of the Almighty behind me. My every thought is motivated by Love and every word expresses this Love. I trust God to speak through me that which needs to be said and at other times I am content to enjoy the blessed peace of stillness. I listen before I speak for my Guidance and afterward have no words to retract or regret. The Spirit of God within me speaks through me in a perfect way to bless, to heal, and uplift all those whom I meet today and every day.

And so it is.

PEACE BEGINS WITH ME

"But now abideth faith, hope, love, these three; and the greatest of these is love." I Cor. 13:13

Love is the answer to world peace. Through Love, I let peace begin with me. I send my love forth to all the world. My thought of love is reflected from one to another until I cannot even conceive of the blessing that started with me.

There is no stranger in a strange land. Love makes all men brothers. Since Love is omnipresent, there is no black hearted criminal, there is no hate-filled despot. Love is all in all, reconciling the world to peace. Love sees good in all and calls forth good in all.

I love God. I love my own individual expression of God. I love my neighbor in every part of the world. I understand him. I bless him. I praise him. I am one with him and he is one with me. Through Love I cast out all thoughts of fear or resentment. Through Love I am unified with all mankind. Love is like a cleansing fire that spreads throughout the world. Let there be Love on earth and let it begin with me.

And so it is.

WORLD PEACE

A TREATMENT FOR WORLD PEACE

"I will now say, Peace be within thee." Ps. 122:8

As Spirit individualized, I am subject only to spiritual Law. I am not alarmed by wars or rumors of wars. "Though an host should encamp against me, my heart shall not fear." Because my faith is in God, I cannot be disturbed. As I accept, in the unity of the Spirit, the Peace of God within me, there will be peace in my world regardless of seeming world conditions. As I recognize the Peace of God within me as the Truth about all men, I give my peace to all mankind. This Peace is the greatest Force in the world. It is, indeed, the only Power and nothing can withstand It. There is no power in conditions; there is only Power in God, a God of Love which is All-Power. Where there is Love there can be no destruction, and God is everywhere Present. As I recognize the Power and Presence of God in all of Life I am a mighty force for the realization of Peace. My daily prayer is LET THY PEACE BE ESTABLISHED IN ME THAT I MAY GIVE IT FORTH TO ALL MANKIND.

And so it is.

FREEDOM NOW

God, at the center of my being, expresses through me. This is the Truth that sets me free. As the seed dies to its old form to rise up into the plant, becoming blossom and fruit, so did I rise up out of my old darkness. I let go of the old life of anxiety and worry. I let go of insecurity and fear. No one is against me.

Now, in that new day, that bright new day when the darkness ceases to be, all gloom is dispelled. I walk out of my prison. Christ in me the hope of glory!

The Perfect Power in me is so great that nothing is impossible to It. I turn from my old life of defeat and inadequacy. I let God express through me as divine right action. I am lifted out of the old life into a new creative experience.

And so it is.

ZEST FOR LIVING

GOD IS LOVING ME NOW

"Behold, what manner of love the Father hath bestowed upon us, that we should be called the sons of God."
I Jn. 3:1

God is loving me now as vitality and strength to do all things. Only my resistance to people and situations makes me tired. As I establish my thoughts in love I am free to call upon my Father for unlimited strength to carry on His work with ease.

God is loving me now, blessing me with Inspiration. I have such zest of accomplishment that my work becomes sheer joy. God's Love is the source of my supply.

God is loving me now through all those who are near and dear to me. Each member of my family and every chance acquaintance is God made manifest in my life. Each one calls forth my love unifying me with His entire creation.

Father, I thank thee that thou hearest me always. I rest in Thy Love.

And so it is.

Addington Books

PSYCHOGENESIS - EVERYTHING BEGINS IN MIND

THE HIDDEN MYSTERY OF THE BIBLE

THE SECRET OF HEALING

THE PERFECT POWER WITHIN YOU

ALL ABOUT GOALS AND HOW TO ACHIEVE THEM

ALL ABOUT PROSPERITY AND HOW YOU CAN PROSPER

THE JOY OF MEDITATION

YOUR NEEDS MET

LIFE NEVER DIES

YOUR MIRACLE BOOK

THE WAY OF HAPPINESS

I AM THE WAY

THE WONDER-WORKING POWER OF GOD

HOW TO LOVE AND BE LOVED